CONTINUALLY AWARE

Rita F. Snowden is widely known in many countries and is the author of more than sixty books for adults and children. After six years in business she trained as a deaconess of the New Zealand Methodist Church, serving in turn two pioneer country areas before moving to the largest city for several years of social work during an economic depression.

Miss Snowden has served the world Church, beyond her own denomination, with regular broadcasting commitments. She has written and spoken in Britain, Canada, the United States, in Australia, and in Tonga at the invitation of Queen Salote. She has represented her church at the World Methodist Conference in Oxford; later being elected the first woman Vice-President of the New Zealand Methodist Church, and President of its Deaconess Association. She is an Honorary Vice-President of the New Zealand Women Writers' Society, a Fellow of the International Institute of Art and Letters, and a member of P.E.N.

Miss Snowden has been honoured by the award of the Order of the British Empire, and by the citation of 'The Upper Room' in America.

Her most recent books are *Prayers for Busy People*, *Christianity Close to Life*, *Bedtime Stories and Prayers* (for children), *I Believe Here and Now*, *Discoveries That Delight*, and *Further Good News*.

RITA F. SNOWDEN

CONTINUALLY AWARE

'It sometimes happens that a familiar verse of the Bible takes on a new meaning; the chance remark of a friend opens a little door in the mind; an unaccountable instinct leads us to worship where we have never been before; a sound, a shape, a touch – and it is like hearing the distant music of church bells over the fields of memory.' These are Dr David H. C. Read's words. Mine are: 'God, help me to be continually aware!'

Collins
FOUNT PAPERBACKS

First published by Fount Paperbacks, London in 1984

© 1984 by Rita F. Snowden

Made and printed in Great Britain by
William Collins Sons & Co. Ltd, Glasgow

DEDICATED TO
our long-time friends
the Rev. Ashleigh Petch,
and his dear wife
Gwen

Contents

Private Rainbows

How long is it since you have seen a rainbow? For years, my favourite poems were nature poems, and my favourite amongst them, Wordsworth's, where he sang:

> My heart leaps up when I behold
> A rainbow in the sky:
> So was it when my life began;
> So is it now I am a man;
> So be it when I shall grow old,
>   Or let me die!

What kind of poem would he have written, I wonder, could he have chanced to see what I saw today? I haven't poetic gifts enough to do it in his stead, but I can tell you about it in prose.

I was flying up from Nelson, in the South Island, when suddenly I saw a rainbow, a *whole* circle, full of colour. It was against a cloud, as we flew – the shadow of our plane itself at its centre – and with surprise a fellow traveller exclaimed: 'Look! A rainbow round the sign of the Cross!'

Wordsworth, poet of the last century, could never have seen it exactly that way, because he was too early to fly; but what he saw, many of his own day missed – as many amongst us miss what God provides of *wonder* and *hope* for our life now. God has, from the very beginning of Time, worked on the refraction of light from the sun upon raindrops. In the very first book of the Bible there is a reference to a new beginning in the life of humanity – after the Flood – *when God set a rainbow in the sky*: 'And God said "This is the token of the covenant which I make between Me and you and every living creature that is with you, for perpetual generations: *I do set My bow in the cloud, and it shall be for a token of a covenant between Me and the earth*"' (Genesis 9:12–13, A.V.).

'In the great old story,' says the commentator in our modern *Interpreter's Bible*, 'Noah did not make the rainbow. God put it there.' So the ground for *wonder and hope* is in God – and we can't live our earth-life without this dual reality.

Knowledge, some say, drives out wonder from the world – but that isn't so. Early in our experience, we learn that wonder and knowledge go hand-in-hand, and worship joins them. 'My heart leaps up', says one person, speaking for us, 'when I behold a rainbow in the sky.' And so does mine! And not only when I am travelling by plane, but also when my feet are solidly on the earth. There are so many natural gifts of God in this world, I find, that move me to wonder. My need is the little prayer I have set in the frontispiece of this present book: 'God help me to be *continually aware*!' Professor Einstein, possessed of one of the greatest minds of our time, puts it well: 'The most beautiful, the most profound emotion we can experience, is the sensation of the mystical. It is the power of all true science. He to whom this emotion is a stranger, *who can no longer wonder*, and stand rapt in awe, is as good as dead . . . This knowledge, this feeling is at the centre of all true religiousness!' This is to say that the kind of experience represented in the love of Nature bestowed by God, is not spoiled by the attrition of time – the wear, the questioning, the struggle of our daily life. Alas for the child, growing to be a teenager, who is not early introduced to this rich wonder. The privilege of being born in the countryside, amid trees and hills, streams and living creatures, is a real gift, before one sets out into the wider world. But we can't all be born in the countryside. One common wonder is that rainbows belong alike to city and countryside.

What G. K. Chesterton feared can happen anywhere: 'The lack of freshness, liveliness must be ascribed to a lack of wonder. The world', he summed up powerfully, 'will never starve for want of wonders, but only for want of wonder.' Wonder brings us face to face with the creative, redemptive love of God in this world – and with our immediate selves. Is there any one of us who has never seen a rainbow? If so, one has nothing but pity to offer him. But, whoever and wherever he is, more pity still must be offered to one to whom a rainbow is offered – but who never allows himself to look up in wonder!

In turn, the commentator of *The Interpreter's Bible* goes on to speak of the world's first rainbow, at the end of the Flood, as a symbol of hope. 'To hope', he adds, 'is defined by Webster as "to cherish a desire with expectation".' Hope has been introduced as having 'a glorious morning face'. It has on-looking, on-going powers, without which we cannot get on in this life. The people – given the first rainbow, as they set out to restore and repeople the earth after the Flood – had to have hope!

And we are their kin, every time we move out from the harsh cold and deluging rains of winter, to dig, and scatter a packet of seeds from a current catalogue. We believe God's words, as He set the first rainbow in the sky: 'I do set My bow in the cloud, and it shall be for a token of a covenant between Me and the earth.' It would never again be totally swept away, as in the Flood. As they set to sow seeds, till, and harvest, and to add a babe to their families every year or so, they remembered God's covenant, and the sign of it, and moved in hope.

And we who put great faith in His promises, do that still.

11

God's world, we believe, in a very enabling way is built on
hope. Darkness gives way to dawn; bleak-flooding winter
to spring; family circles re-established with every little
child; with an unimaginable Life beyond what we call
Death.

We pray, in the words of Charles Strong's hymn:

> Reveal Thyself in words by wisdom wrought,
> In ever wakening, every deepening thought,
> In *rainbow hopes* which span earth's dreariest hour,
> In lowly love's all-conquering, God-like power.

So in between – in the course of our stay in this world,
mingling with others, doing our work, moving about as the
seasons, with their opportunities, come and go – further
wonder-ful, and hope-ful experiences come to us.

After all, this is God's world! There is no forgetting
Tischendorf's find, in the remote monastery of St
Catherine on Mount Sinai. A teacher from Leipzig, he set
off into that locality, to seek out, in monasteries and tombs,
scraps of early manuscript. On the first evening of his
arrival at the monastery, whilst scarcely begun on his
search, his eye fell on a fuel-bucket near a fireplace.
Turning over mouldy and torn manuscripts put out because
they were of no value, he suddenly observed several pages
written in Greek uncials. And his former long-time study
told him that these were of value: part of forty-three pages
of one of the oldest known manuscripts of the New
Testament, later to be known as the *Codex Sinaiticus*. It
took fifteen years to complete the search for this world
treasure. But of that first night, of the first find,
Tischendorf wrote: 'At that moment the world turned
upside down in my head, *and I saw all the colours of the
rainbow*!'

That's it – wonder and hope, inexplicably tied!

12

A Tonic of Big Things

I had some minutes to spare in the doctor's waiting room today. Not long, but long enough to feel gratitude that I was born in this century. Had I been born in the last, not to mention the sixteenth or the seventeenth, I would have died from the heart condition that I've carried through the years. Now, I leave each time with an adequate prescription, though I marvel that my old chemist can ever read what is scrawled thereon.

I've always been interested in Dr Deryck Brand's treatment of the Honourable Jane Campion – it was so unusual. Somebody hinted that perhaps she needed a tonic; and in time, her doctor attended to that. 'Here is a prescription for you', he said: *'See a few big things!'* And he went on to urge her to travel, to see Niagara Falls. 'Go for the big things!' he repeated. 'You will like to remember, when you are bothering about pouring water in and out of teacups, Niagara is flowing still!'

I know what he means, for I have been to Niagara, and there is no least doubt about what Dr Brand claimed. Happily, I got there with no prompting from my doctor – my need was not of that kind. (But year by year, I am told, some two million people come from the ends of the earth to gaze upon that mighty volume of water, constantly, gloriously flowing! A Jesuit missionary was the first to gaze upon it, back in 1678, though by then another had told of its thundering sound, without sight of it.)

Mighty Niagara, of course, is not the only 'Big Thing' to lead its viewer to a healing sense of perspective – there is the Grand Canyon. I had flown over its immense gorge sculpted by the Colorado River; but it was chiefly when I approached the Canyon at foot-level, and moved about its immense rim, measured in miles each way, that its majesty met me. And I heard of its 'bigness', and saw its changing colours, till the sun went down in gentle blues and mauves, pinks, cinnabar-reds and golds. The river that runs through it looks like a thread, seen from the air; and the powers of sun, wind and rain do what the Creator wills. A distinguished geologist claims: 'It is a spectacle unrivalled on earth!'

In my home country, we have the Sutherland Falls – not so wonderful as Niagara, but beautifully, generously flowing. At one time, they used to be celebrated as 'the world's tallest waterfalls', but that honour is now held by Venezuela's 'Angel Falls' at three thousand two hundred and twelve feet. I have carried my pack to the base of Sutherland Falls – along the Milford Track, through our mighty, tall, tree-blessed mountains – and it still causes me to wonder!

Among other 'Big Things' in our small country are our impressive State Kauri-trees – immense trees, raising their heads up into the skies. Experts say they were considerable trees two thousand years ago, when the Cross went up on Calvary. The biggest of them today is *Tane Mahutu*: thirteen metres in girth, with its lowest branches some twelve metres from the ground. I have stood in silence beneath this 'Big Thing', and it puts much else into perspective.

We have, of course, no tall structures like America's Empire State Building, which is one hundred and two storeys high. When I ascended to its viewing platform at the end of the day, its bigness and its beauty as the sun went down and ten thousand thousand lights came out below us, were unforgettable!

Yet I must say that natural things move me more. No

man can match the creativeness of God, and there are so many 'Big Things' of His making in this world of ours! We need never lack a tonic of big things. If we can't travel, we can go out under the stars, or lift up our eyes to the hills. And then there is the sea!

The big things of Nature and the works of men's hands are not all – not by any means: there is God Himself. We see Him revealed in the Bible in both Old and New Testaments, but especially in the New. Yet some do not read it.

Dr J. B. Phillips, in our day, moved by our need, wrote a widely read book for the Epworth Press, my first London publishers, titled *Your God is Too Small*. A striking title! 'The trouble with many people today', he began, 'is that they have not found *a God big enough for modern needs*. While their experience of life has grown in a score of directions, and their mental horizons have been expanded to the point of bewilderment, by world events and by scientific discoveries, their ideas of God have remained largely static. It is obviously impossible for an adult to worship the conception of God that exists in the mind of a child . . . If, by a great effort of will, he does do this, he will always be secretly afraid lest some new truth may expose the juvenility of his faith.'

For it is from God that all these 'Big Things' come. He from Whom we get our lasting values, our sustaining thoughts and ideas. Early in my Christian experience, I came upon a little verse prayer:

> Father,
> If I could only see the difference
> Between the *really big things and little things*!
> I do not ask for better – or for more –
> I only ask for this: '*God keep my soul*
> *From growing petty!*'

This prayer can only be addressed to 'the Big God', Maker of heaven and earth, men and women in all their diversity, creatures, and all that is – unmatched, even in this age of outward moon-probes, X-rays, probing within, world-flight, and other developments that leave most of us gasping. Long before our Space Age, one sang:

> If I ascend up into Heaven, Thou art there,
> If I make my bed in Hell, behold Thou art there.
> If I take the wings of the morning,
> And dwell in the uttermost parts of the sea:
> Even there shall Thy hand lead me,
> And Thy right hand shall hold me.
>
> Psalm 139:8–9, A.V.

This glorious conception of God is still very supportive. But we have more in the New Testament. God's Son, asked by one of His disciples, 'What is God like?', could only answer: 'Have I been so long time with you, and yet hast thou not known Me, Philip? *He that hath seen Me hath seen the Father!*' (John 14:9, A.V.). In other words, 'What I am in Time, that God is eternally.'

A. E. Whitham, sensitive and beloved modern-day Methodist preacher, brought it forward for us, beautifully and challengingly: 'He is a God, not standing afar off, waiting for us to draw nigh, but a God who sought us out, striving ever to enter, trying the doors, strategically planning, making Himself small as a child and lying down on the doorstep of the world, until the world, moved by the cry of a child . . . took the child in, and unwittingly let God through . . . A God who would forgive sin when you asked and because you asked, ready to forgive even righteous people if they would ask . . . Not concerned with rewards and punishments, like a typical ruler, *but only with right*

16

relations like a true Father!'

God is, we find, a self-disclosing God. That is what we have learned from Jesus's ministry: His enduring Love. There is nothing in God petty or out-of-scale with the immensities of our world and our century, its knowledge, and its deepest needs. Teilhard de Chardin is right: 'We must have a vision of God commensurate with an expanding universe.' Only a small child, hearing early Old Testament stories at bedtime, could have exclaimed: 'Mummy, God must have been more exciting then!' (No, little one, No, that isn't so – and as you grow older, read more, think more, experience more. I hope you will discover it!)

Amazing Grace

What time of night it was, or how long I'd been asleep, I'd no idea. Then I heard steps on the stairs of the country inn where I was staying, high up beyond the town. Suddenly, finding myself awake in the velvety darkness, I snicked on the light. It was a quarter of an hour short of midnight. So I decided to stay awake.

It was years since I had celebrated the closing of the last day of an Old Year and the coming-in of the New. It seemed best to put out the light again – and soon I was glad I had. Experiences that come to one alone, and in the darkness, always seem more memorable.

As the minutes ticked by, I heard further footsteps on the road that went by, and further restrained voices of men, women and young folk. And it dawned upon me that they were having a country gathering, not too far away. There, I knew, were kindly trees encircling a flat welcoming place. I listened. Cheers, and the ringing of a bell told me when we reached midnight. A further chatteration of voices followed, then there was more singing.

But what was most impressive, after a telling pause, was the effort of an unknown Scot in their company, who took up his pipes, and there suddenly played John Newton's *Amazing Grace*! As the hinge of the Old and the New Years, in the darkness that provided our setting, it was unforgettable!

The tune has become widely known in the last few years; though I am not sure that so many know its message, or the story of the composer's glorious transformation! John Newton was, in his early life, a questionable character.

Impressed into the rough naval service of the times, he became in turn a slave-dealer. Men were counted no better than animals – it was a merciless existence. Many of them died before reaching their destination.

But a day came when the profligate found himself confronted by a new Master. Turning from slave-driving, Newton took a job as tide-surveyor in the great maritime city of Liverpool. But that did not wholly satisfy him. Soon, more and more under the Gospel of Christ, he knew himself to be under Divine Grace, and he began, by degrees, to preach, and to write hymns. Among a cluster of his favourites, sung to this day all round the world, are: 'How sweet the Name of Jesus sounds', 'Glorious things of Thee are spoken', and this one which came to me with such power: 'Amazing Grace.' (I can only hope that it moved as powerfully that unseen company that night, as the pipes spoke out!)

A transformed character, Newton became in time an ordained preacher, in charge of a church. London got to know him very well. He never tried to boast of his personal history of misdoing, rejoicing rather in what he referred to as 'Amazing Grace'. He actually fashioned his own epitaph – and very honestly. He lived to bring glory to his Lord and Saviour. When I returned home early in the New Year, I made it my business to take down a book on my study shelves, and from there I copied his words:

JOHN NEWTON, Clerk,
Once an infidel and libertine;
A servant of slaves in Africa:
Was by the rich mercy of our Lord and Saviour
Jesus Christ,
Preserved, restored, pardoned,
And appointed to preach the Faith
He had long laboured to destroy . . .

And this mastery of a man's life, transforming it, making it a gracious and serviceable thing, is no ancient story, to be proclaimed by the pipes at midnight. It is still as effective, given the same reception, in a wilful man's heart. Dietrich Bonhoeffer (in our day of clashing leaders and obligations), young thinker, teacher of German pastors, opponent of the Nazis in all their ramifications, was in time driven into the dark, cruel days of the concentration camp, and eventually martyred. One of his favourite warnings – in the days when he could speak his mind freely – was against what he called 'Cheap Grace'. What did he mean? Something completely opposite to that transforming power granted to John Newton.

The word 'Grace', in our language, is a very beautiful and telling word. The Old Testament delights to speak of God as *gracious* – 'a God ready to pardon, gracious and merciful' (turn up Nehemiah 9:17, A.V., or Psalm 111:4, A.V.: 'The Lord is *gracious* and full of compassion').

'But the beautiful word "Grace"', as Dr C. F. Hunter likes to remind me, 'is more distinctive of the New Testament. It is used, of course, in Classical Greek for gracefulness of person or of movement, and for the graciousness of a superior towards his inferiors. *But in the New Testament it is consecrated . . . and is reserved exclusively for the free and undeserved mercy of God.*'

This is the 'Amazing Grace' – through Christ – which John Newton, in his frustrated, cruel, miserable life came to know.

This is the 'Amazing Grace' – through Christ – which Dietrich Bonhoeffer rejoiced in, over against 'Cheap Grace'.

'Grace is not something that God *has* to give us – but a gift that He *wants* to give us; it is Love's extra, surpassing here and now, all human limitations, exceeding all deserts!'

We are reminded Sunday by Sunday of this reality, as the words of the Benediction come to our ears as worship closes: '*The Grace of our Lord Jesus Christ*' is the oft-repeated blessing. Paul in his day, in his letters, used it all through his transformed ministry, as did John Newton, glorying in it. Sometimes Paul elaborated it a little. Not to change the reality, but only to make it more understandable. In Romans 16:20, A.V., his words are: 'The Grace of our Lord Jesus Christ be with you. Amen.' In Romans 16:24, A.V., this is lengthened by one word: 'The Grace of our Lord Jesus Christ be with you *all*. Amen.' Paul can think of no gift better to have God bestow upon his loved friends; and he repeats his longings, exactly (Philippians 4:23, A.V.). Slightly abbreviated, he writes it into his letter to the Corinthians (16:23, A.V.). He sometimes has good reason to admonish them for one thing or another; sometimes even to judge them. But he never at any time leaves them without 'the Grace of the Lord Jesus Christ' – for he knows that they cannot know the fulness of the Christian life in this daily setting, without it.

Nor can we! So we welcome it again, recorded in 1 Thessalonians 5:28, A.V., and again in 2 Thessalonians 3:18. And no one of us can hear it too often. Our only trouble is that, when we do read it very often and hear it spoken as a benediction very often, we become casual, and some of the glory goes out of the reality. This is something we have to guard against – as did the first followers of our Risen Lord, his friends to whom Paul wrote so wisely, so warmly.

One nearer our own century put this reality into words to be sung to God the Father – and very far-reaching words they are!

> His every word of Grace is strong
> As that which built the skies;

Continually Aware

The Voice that rolls the stars along
Speaks all the promises!

Do you feel that, as you take leave of the place of worship?
I can say that this year it meant to me a very great deal, as
I moved in the darkness of midnight, from night to day,
from the Old Year to the New!

Worthwhile Work

Occasionally a letter mid-morning brings me excitement, and it was so this morning. Some years ago, I wrote for young people a true story about a carpenter who came out from Scotland with his kit of tools, to make his way in this country. And this morning's letter was a sequel to it. It came from the Manager of 'Ross Home', a long-established centre for retired folk. Many reach the point, these days, when they can no longer manage in their own homes, and Dunedin is well served by 'Ross Home'. My good friends, Miss Betty and her aged sister, have not long moved in. During the years of our close friendship, we have exchanged visits and many letters. Always we have enjoyed good talk and laughter, not forgetting current news of the Church.

But lately there have been gaps, and I fell to wondering whether one or other was unwell – it might even be that kindly Death had caught up with them. But no! In a neat letter, over the signature of the Manager, Mr William C. L. Christie, I learned that both were well. And with thanks for my enquiry, he assured me of his gladness of this link, since he had many times retold my carpenter story to the young folk in Dunedin city and countryside whom he addressed for the Presbyterian Social Service Association. 'Though, till now', he added, 'I've not sought out your address, to acknowledge it to its writer.'

My striking story found its point in the fine southern city of Dunedin. But James Fletcher – Sir James, as we remember him now – did not stay there. Soon, his name was being raised on other builders' boards above the deep foundations of buildings.

And Fletcher became a well-known name in New Zealand's northern and largest city – rising taller and taller on its sea-blessed rim. Mechanical aids of immense size were increasingly available, and the Fletcher fleet of yellow lorries was growing. It was all hard work – and James Fletcher was now a married man, Time bringing children about his knees.

But nothing could spoil the relevancy of 'the secret' that his father, at leave-taking years before, had entrusted to him: *'Never build a job you've to run past!'* (As I read through that nice letter this morning, I was to find coincidentally that the first building Fletcher put up in the country of his adoption, was 'Ross Home'. And he has never had to run past it; indeed, he made a long journey south, the length of the land, to attend its fiftieth anniversary in 1968, and with joy shared with all involved in that long-to-be-remembered occasion.)

'Why', I ask myself, 'is work so important – not just carpentering or building? Is it because God, our Creator-builder wants it? Or because He wants us?'

Of one reality there is no misjudging: when He settled His human-divine Son among men and women of earth, He gave Him a full measure of meaningful work. He set Him down in the little town of Nazareth, to be a manual worker, 'a Good Worker'!

And He did a sound piece of work there – no one can raise any doubt about that. No man of the soil there expressed dissatisfaction when he yoked his beasts; no housewife drew unhappy attention to moths that had crept under 'the lid of her wedding-chest where she kept her linen. When Jesus was ready to start what is called His public ministry, He did not hesitate to do it amongst His one-time customers who knew the quality of His work in the past. None of it contradicted the message of His public preaching. Choosing timbers from the forest; sweating over foundations of buildings raised; planing; fashioning door frames; and setting shelves; added to smoothly fashioned ox-yokes, and gracefully lidded linen-chests, no one could ever charge Him, on His return, with a shabby job. He wasn't afraid to start His preaching and healing where people knew Him!

I reflected on this with great satisfaction, as I walked the modest streets between the workshops of present-day Nazareth. Carpenter-builders still work there as did He, with the sweet-smelling, curly wood-shavings about sandalled feet.

The place did not much matter, where the Son of God rendered up the result of His daily work – it was the quality of the work He did that mattered, all with good taste, exactitude, and skill. Nothing was ever good enough for Him to show to a customer, unless it was fit to show to God! He had never any reason to 'run past' what He had done.

One of our day's most thoughtful and sensitive of His followers – Evelyn Underhill – has persuaded us that once our spirit is right, any setting will suit. Said she: 'What was done in the Carpenter's Shop, can be done in *the engineer's shop*.' Indeed, no amount of regular churchgoing on Sunday will compensate for functional inefficiency in what we offer to God, and our fellows, during the week.

To make our fullest offering, we soon learn that we must keep ourselves fit, as Jesus did. For nothing can suggest that He allowed Himself to become the frail, slim, white-faced leader some of the pictures of the medieval artists and later craftsmen in stained glass allowed to come to us. If He had been that piously frail, He could never have done the daily work He did, nor known the meaning of honest sweat. God's word at His baptism was, 'This is My beloved Son, in whom I am well pleased' (Matthew 3:17, A.V.).

'Work satisfaction' is a good modern-day term, that we ought each to know something of – but in itself, it isn't enough. God is involved in all work. I love the way Dr William Temple, the relatively young Archbishop of Canterbury of our century, put it for us: 'God is not interested only in pulpits and preachers, hassocks and hymnbooks! He cares for carpenters, for typists and chemists and cooks, for farmers and gardeners, and teachers, and doctors.' (I like the way he starts with carpenters.) It became very precious to me when I spent a whole day in Hong Kong, in the little 'Church of the Holy Carpenter', set in the midst of working people; open every day of the week; its altar fashioned out of a carpenter's bench. Those who worshipped there knew only too well what hard work meant – and what satisfaction! The likeness of the Holy Carpenter, chastely carved by one of their number, is at eye-level, reminding them of His close presence and His redemption of the common task. They worship God – even as He did – not only with spoken words, but with toil of sinew, muscle and skill.

> This is the miracle I seek,
> O living Christ,
> Your strength and purpose in my hands,
> Your kindness in my voice,
> Within my heart Your certainty of God,
> Your love for all mankind.
>
> Anon.

The Clear Call

Before I glimpsed the Sea of Galilee, or walked along its shores, I heard a distinguished traveller say: 'It is the loveliest lake in the world. Its lapping waves, in calm times, speak out its name, "Gal-i-lee"!' It is something of a surprise to find Luke always referring to it in his gospel as the 'lake' of Galilee, never 'the sea'. But then, it is small – only thirteen miles long, and eight from east to west. In a comfortable shape among the hills, its surface lies six hundred and eighty feet below sea-level; and lying in a genial climate, its surrounding countryside is beautifully fertile. Only when sudden storms beat down from between the hills is the surface disturbed – and then moods of a dangerous nature present themselves.

In early times, Josephus the historian recorded as many as nine populous cities round its shores. When I sought lodging, I found Tiberias the most important – though not very big. In His day, Jesus's continual need was to seek out for Himself small, uncrowded places.

Many of His friends lived hereabouts; many of them fishermen. And it was to them that His 'clear call' rang out, in the immortal words: '*Follow Me!*' Dr William Barclay wrote for us a little book, *The Master's Men*, and therein underlined: 'Peter was a Galilean, and a typical Galilean.' As a fisherman the Lake was a familiar expanse of water; he knew all its moods, and the hills were never any distance off. By day, as now, they were bluey-green, merging into brown, golden as the day closed. I sought out a position from which I could embrace the scene's simplicity. Nothing can have altered those hills – they must still be much as Jesus knew them and loved them.

I visualize Peter and his fellow fishermen as good, sensible, industrious fellows. In their time, there were several methods of fishing: by line; by the casting-net, from the edge of the Lake, with a circular movement; together with boat-fishing, by the dragnet, with a rope from each corner.

With my friend, I found I had other links with Peter, as we were taken to the far side of the Lake by a present-day Galilean. At lunchtime, after we had parted from him, we shared a simple meal from a fish called 'Peter's Perch', *mousht* in the Arabic.

Returning, we travelled by land, round the curving shore in an old bus. We wanted to be close to the people – and we certainly were, a fact that affords me a chuckle still, as I look back beyond my colour photographs. I see the imposing passenger next me, who, in order to have his hands free to buy his ticket, set down his leather business satchel at his feet – and out of the gap each end appeared the head of a fine white duck, one looking east, one west.

But that was not all! A peasant then mounted the bus steps with a generous load of ripe melons, gathered up into a striped sheet. But it was hard, in the crowded bus, to place them. They were too large to settle properly in the rack where he set them; and as the bus lurched, down they came – and cracked! He returned them; but the juice trickled through on to those travellers in the aisles!

These experiences only made Jesus very near, very real. He often found Himself in crowds, and being jostled. His first fishermen disciples were at their work when they heard His 'clear call', '*Follow Me! And I will make you fishers of men!*' (Matthew 4:19, A.V.). I can't think that that was the first time they had looked into His eyes; or the first time

28

they had heard that clear sure voice. At any rate, those words stirred their best selves!

(Socrates, long before, in like spirit challenged an ordinary listener, and received the reply: 'I have nothing, but I give you myself.' Socrates' immediate words were: 'Do you not see that you are giving me the most precious gift of all?')

That was how Jesus set Christian values beside the shimmering Lake of Galilee, or 'Sea'. It makes no difference. It is the nature of Jesus's call to men and women of all times that matters!

At first, some said that those good, honest fishermen, who buckled on their sandals, and went with Him into towns and villages, and eventually into the world, were 'unlearned and ignorant men'. But that was true only in the literal sense that they had not been trained in any sacred school. They had skills, nevertheless, and experiences. They were men of body, mind and spirit, by no means merely 'yes-men'.

They were prepared to tie up their boats. Following would be exciting, but it called for courage, too. With the years, it would cost some of them their lives. Following this new Master was not just a matter of walking about the countryside in long, cool garments, mingling with the people who gave them welcome; resting under the sky at day's end; and sleeping round the campfire at night. It was to take their young Master, and themselves sometimes, away from their families. It was a supreme spiritual adventure, that in time would mark the world with a Cross! And it is still, since those glorious words *'Follow Me!'* echoing the world around!

We have now to buckle on the sandals of our spirits. I shall never cease to be thankful that I was led to do this in my lively teens, and I shall continue during the whole of my brief minute of Time on this earth, as a member of His on-going Church!

One of the earliest post-biblical disciples to answer His clear call was Justin Martyr (AD 100–165). 'After our conversion', he was glad to say, 'we who devoted ourselves to the arts of magic, now consecrate ourselves to the good and unbegotten God; we who loved above all else the ways of acquiring riches and possessions, now hand over to a community fund what we possess, and share it with every needy person; we who hated and killed one another and would not share our hearth with those of another tribe . . . *after the coming of Christ*, live together with them, and pray for our enemies, and try to convince those who hate us unjustly, so that they who live according to the good commands of Christ, may have a firm hope of receiving the same reward as ourselves from God, who governs all.'

From the day our Master walked the shores of little Galilee, calling His followers, Peter, James, John and the rest, till the day that clear call came to us, He has been working wonders through ordinary men and women. And still 'the clear call' rings out; and others will take up my prayer:

> As Thou didst call by Galilee, O Lord, I have heard Thee down the long shore of the years;
> With up-raised faces and responsive heart, I have come to join my discipleship to that of Peter, James and John.
> I have chosen Thee, and Thy way of Life – not because I must – but with all the kingdoms of the earth in sight.
> *In the quietness, and during the busy demanding hours of day – my whole life through – Master, hold me true! Have for Thine own best ends, my own best energies. AMEN.*

A Glad Response

It was a new experience for me, and new for those who had called me to it. I had not broadcast before, had not shared the things of my heart and mind with an *unseen* audience, though I had spoken much in public. I was asked to do a weekly session in our country's largest city. But there was, as yet, no studio prepared; so I had to stand in a space made in a music-dealer's showroom of pianos, cornets, drums and cellos.

As time went on, I moved to a little glassed-in studio; and looking out from my solitary existence, made me feel like a goldfish. But I could now sit; and no longer trembled at the knees. Wednesday by Wednesday morning, I made my way into the city's heart. My session was not a musical one – as my first setting may have suggested – but one set to strengthen and cheer ordinary mortals, sponsored by the Mission where I served.

Those were hard times. Amidst a country-wide economic crisis the realities of the Christian Faith that prompted my social service were daily put to the test.

I tried to visualize where my listeners would be at that hour – presupposing that I had listeners, though for several weeks I had no proof of that. It was not like a public utterance in a hall or church; for that I had trained myself to speak without dependence on my notes so that I could look into the faces of those before me. To be able to do that was a wonderful inspiration – it was how I got my response.

With broadcasting, and – sometimes with a chuckle – I shared my mind and heart with persons unseen, living alone, taking a cup of coffee at that hour; or enjoying a pipe on a garden-seat after an hour's digging; or busy as a young mother feeding her baby; or a convalescing grandmother at her knitting in bed. There might be also, I thought, a workman at his bench. But I couldn't be sure. And week after week, I finished my brief sharing, and came out on to the street again, to find everything looked just the same: the same pedestrians hustled by; the same shop windows showed their wares; the same traffic noises mounted. Had anybody heard me? I couldn't be sure – and it was a bit dispiriting. Then suddenly, at a street corner, I met a visiting countryman staying at a hotel for a couple of days whilst up on business. We knew each other well, and his eyes brightened. 'I've just been listening to you, and it's been the best thing, so far, since I came up to town.' And, as you can well believe, my eyes brightened, too: *I had got my essential response.*

(Soon, friendly letters and phone calls began to come – and I've never lost my love for broadcasting *to the great unseen*, as I have opportunity – the situation the same everywhere: in Auckland, in Wellington, Rotorua, Sydney, Melbourne, Adelaide, London.)

So much in human relationship hangs on response. I don't any longer ignore the four capital letters at the foot of any invitation card that comes to me through the post: R.S.V.P. And a little while ago, I saw the same law operating when, within half a minute of finishing a colour TV interview, my phone rang, and an appreciative friend was at the other end.

For fourteen years, as some of the readers of this book will know, I contributed to a long-established British weekly – and there are a good many Thursdays in fourteen years. Wet and fine, at home or abroad, with varied obligations, in illness and in health. I never missed an issue; though all the time, I knew the nature of journalism, even Christian journalism. A day or two after one's precious article appears, in many instances, the paper is discarded to wrap up vegetables at the little corner shop, or a collection of domestic rubbish in some kitchen. But from time to time, a reader somewhere is helped by something I have written, and writes from the ends of the earth, to tell me so. *There is a response – and that makes all the difference.* The same can be said when I have laboured eagerly, but at greater length, to write a book – and I have written many, some now in translation, some in Braille, some in Talking Books. From time to time, the 'postie' continues his share of my on-going ministry of encouragement, and drops letters into my box, many of them bearing strange and beautiful stamps.

Occasionally, a reader whom I have never met – save in my writing – arrives from some distant country, where I have never been, and steps over my doorstep. This is not to claim more than many another can claim, but it is a strengthening reality.

Being the human beings we are, we cannot fully or forever give out what we have to add to life, without some response. Naomi Jacob underlined this in her book *Me – Yesterday and Today*. Of a favourite story of hers, that she had shared time and again in speech, she had to admit: 'To put over what you believe to be something really funny, and to be met with a deathly silence. That is perhaps why broadcasting, unless you have a live audience, is to me so difficult.' (She might have been speaking of an occasional hall full of people.) 'There is one reaction', she says of those experiences hard to forget. 'As they say, "You work your eyebrows off", and you have no idea what the listeners are thinking or feeling.'

Others, with rich things to share, on occasion make a similar discovery. When Jacques Gordon was first violinist in the Chicago Symphony Orchestra, he stood one day for two hours, to test this out, on one of the city's busiest streets, and played his priceless violin. The finest music, by one of the finest musicians, meant nothing to many who made up the crowds that day – they saw him, they heard him, and passed him in utter unconcern.

Even our Lord knew this kind of experience. He spoke winsomely to a company of adults, and one of them happened to be Matthew the New Testament scribe who later wrote it down (Matthew 11:16–17, A.V.). And Jesus's words are full of meaning. He had seen the children playing in the marketplace, some at weddings, some at funerals, and He recalled their reactions: 'We have piped unto you, and you have not danced', and later, 'We have mourned unto you, and you have not lamented.' In other words: 'We've tried everything, and *ye have offered us no response.*'

As He mingled day by day with the people about Him, He likened them to those children. And it showed most painfully in His own beloved Jerusalem, with Time running out. As He stood, thoughtfully overlooking the city where so much was at stake, He had to cry: 'O Jerusalem, Jerusalem . . . How often would I have gathered thy children together, even as a hen gathereth her chickens under her wings, *and ye would not*' (Matthew 23:37, A.V.). Of course. He could never bring Himself to *force* any one – each had freely to offer a glad response!

During my unforgettable visit to Winchester Cathedral, I recalled H. V. Morton's visit there. He tells how he was taken up into the tower with a small mixed party under the guidance of the verger. The verger carefully numbered them, then gave each a bellrope. Pointing to each by number as he had need of his or her contribution, he managed to bring forth the hymn tune of 'Abide with me'.

Morton's wise comment was: 'We were delighted with

ourselves; but of course, it wasn't music. (They all did what they were told, and *you can't get music by commandment*.') Neither can you get Love, or Fellowship, or Service – *and these are three lasting responses that Christ desires of us*!

Blessed Be Sleep

Sometimes, I lie awake, but not often! Kindly Sleep has found me in countless homes the world round, and also in hotels, hostels and inns.

The gracious city of Gloucester offered me a treasurable experience. Long before dusk, having finished time within the Cathedral and about, I found myself at the entrance of The New Inn, in Northgate Street. Its name fascinated me, before I had time so much as to step into its old-fashioned courtyard, with its three-sided balcony served by ascending steps, or accept the little bedroom offered me above. The New Inn must have been *new* at one time – but that was plainly long ago. I found it now had an uneven, oaken floor, and that things dropped tended to run away to a far corner.

After I had finished my evening meal, I turned to my Beckinsale's *Companion into Gloucestershire*. There was a rewarding and lengthy comment on the Cathedral. Then I found the author saying: 'The New Inn in Northgate Street is among the dozen oldest hostels in England, having been built about 1455 by John Twining, a monk of the Abbey. Originally intended to house pilgrims to the shrine of Edward II, it has kept the ancient balconies around its courtyard.'

Much has changed since 1455. 'A pilgrim' from the other side of the world, I now parked my little car, instead of a pair of dust-laden sandals and a stout stick. But later, as I lay under The New Inn's hospitable roof, I doubted very much whether 'God's Good Gift of Sleep' had changed at all. 'O Sleep', someone long ago had said, 'it is a gentle thing, beloved from Pole to Pole!'

Our present-day world, of course, is noisier, swifter moving, by day and by night. And adults still take a little time to drop off to sleep – more, of course, in unfamiliar situations, and when assailed by the day's activities, wearinesses and worries.

'During our infancy,' as Robert Lynd, the essayist, reminds us, 'all the world is in conspiracy to persuade us to sleep; but during the rest of our lives, all the world is in a conspiracy to persuade us to wake up.' So we have to learn to do a good deal about it, for ourselves. I have among my friends several who can manage with as little as four hours' sleep nightly, but I am not one such; I belong to those who commonly count on eight. Respectful enquiry reveals how many, as the years advance, enjoy a brief nap during the daytime (as did Winston Churchill, one of our busiest of busy persons).

I don't know how our Queen manages; but the first Queen Elizabeth carried her own bed with her, as part of her entourage, when she travelled. I have never had occasion to do that, I'm glad to say – or I couldn't have circled the earth several times, and slept, and wakened so many times, so refreshingly.

Some people won't sleep in a strange bed unless its head is to the north; others won't sleep on a mattress that has been turned on a Friday, if they know about it. Others again insist on a hard bed; and some must be assured of a soft pillow. During my lecture itineraries I have slept on every possible kind of bed: hard, soft, short, long, downstairs, upstairs, within the quiet of surrounding countryside, or near a railway in some ambitious town, with noisy shunting going on all night long, in cities with road traffic, including long-distance lorries bearing loads to sleeping merchants. Grinding gears show no would-be sleeper any mercy; nor do motorbikes, hill-climbing, in the hours of night.

Writing in his *Human Psychology*, Dr Kenneth Walker reminds us 'Sleep is the means by which nerve-cells recover from their fatigue, and since most of us spend a third of our lives – eight hours nightly – asleep, we are naturally interested in it.'

Professors and doctors our world round, are still engaged in experiments to discover what more can be known about Sleep, and not only the difference between those of us who are light sleepers and those of us who can justly claim to be sound sleepers. A little while ago a clutch of students at Colgate University gave themselves up to a special study of Sleep. They embraced a number of questions. Each was asked to wear a mask fitted so that it could measure and analyse the air breathed whilst wearing it. And a second instrument recorded a sleeper's blood pressure. Nor was that all: an infra-red camera recorded all the unconscious twists and turns of the 'patient' during a night's sleep. Some were found to affect as many as thirty different positions.

Sleep – that so many of us take so much for granted – sounds, in broad daylight, when these learned ones have finished their tests, very surprising.

But, along with these experts, *we always need a man, a woman of essential Faith*. 'Sleep is God's Gift!' The Psalmist found pleasure in reminding himself and his fellows of that reality. 'God's gifts', said he, 'come to His loved ones, as they sleep' (Psalm 127:2, Moffatt). And we know how wonderful many of these gifts are!

> New every morning is the love
> Our waking and up-rising prove,
> Through Sleep and darkness safely brought,
> Restored to life and power and thought.

Sleep – even if we could know all about it – is God's Good Gift, a constant miracle. Though you and I have always, it seems, *to co-operate in its sweet, natural, supportive flow*. A regular set bedtime can help, if it is a feature of our lifetime, without much variance.

And an interest in 'bed-bookery' at day's end is a help, as well as a great joy. For myself, I feel that a bedroom without a shelf of books is a poor haven at day's end. I welcomed the words of no less an authority than Dr W. A. R. Thomson, editor of *The Practitioner*, and learned medical correspondent of *The Times*, when I came upon them. 'Half an hour's quiet reading in bed', he claimed, 'is almost a better sedative than all the barbiturates in the world.'

Of course, one needs to choose one's books for bedtime, carefully – nothing too exciting! But the book world is full of titles that have power to ease one gently from the frustrations and wearinesses of the day past, creating an atmosphere of peace for one's pillow. Sometimes, it is a pleasant travel book that will serve, guiding one gently off into loved countries and cities where one has been, and found delight; or a book telling of where one has not been – or indeed, might never go. But its wide spaces and misty passes are full of fascination, thanks to Freya Stark and a handful of good travellers who are able to share their travels with us. So now we can travel in comfort, and on the horizontal.

At another time, one may welcome an autobiography, racily, sensitively written, the offering of someone whom one hardly knows – but would like to know. Or it might be a novel – though, I confess, it is never easy to find enough good ones. I'm not interested at bedtime (if ever) in 'the cleverness of the clever', nor the on-going emotional details of one who goes on for five hundred or so pages. It is not enough to question: 'Did she get him in the end?' Or

'Was she happy?' 'Was he?' I don't always stay the distance necessary to make that discovery.

And there are other books still – devotional books. I have actually written some myself – one lately on a fresh approach to the Psalms, *Discoveries That Delight*, because I've often longed to resort to just such a book at nightfall.

Both Great and Small

I had not been long in the great city of Liverpool when, in a side street, I came upon a builder. He was making a play-hut. His head was down to the task in hand, though he seemed to have only box-wood to work with. I stopped, to show more than a passing interest – and he told me he was ten. I wondered where his father was that Saturday, and what he would have to say about the use of his saw and hammer when he came back.

I had never been in Liverpool before, and it seemed fitting that within the first few minutes I should come upon 'a builder', even though only ten. I had come all the way up from London especially to see the work of another builder. No name known to me was more famous than that of Giles-the-builder, or if you insist on his full name, Sir Giles Gilbert Scott, builder of the great cathedral. It stands high, its great tower at the top of the hill, above the houses and shops. I had no need to ask my way – nobody could miss it.

When first its builder dreamed of it, working eagerly and skilfully, he was only twenty-three. He put in for a current competition – as did many others, from many places – and his dream was eventually accepted.

It was, of course, thrilling for a young man with his skills to have the chance to build a cathedral. He had need to give it much more thought, as the weeks and months passed, and meanwhile set himself to gather about him others who could help. The steep site had to be cleared, the foundation dug, and gradually the walls and the mighty tower arose.

It was, by degrees, seen to be a thing of balance and beauty of form.

Every part of the building had to be chiselled out of stone. Within, it was so spacious that when finished, three thousand people could join in worship without any pillars getting in their way. And it was a wonderful day, when it was finished and officially opened: the altar ready, with its Cross; the bishop's throne in place; the baptismal font; the pews, the chapels, the memorials set; the stained-glass windows in scarlet and gold, rich blue, and purples and greens!

Her Royal Highness, Princess Elizabeth – now our beloved Queen – journeyed north to open the massive doors. And the people entered in. There was great joy, and no wonder! It was a new cathedral, magnificently set, unlike any other in all England – and built to the glory of God!

Some day I shall go again to Liverpool. In the meantime, *I rejoice in those in our age, who can undertake such great tasks!*

But that is only half the story, *and in Liverpool both halves are held in beautiful balance*, the great and the small. Not everybody, I find, knows that Sir Giles, who designed that magnificent cathedral, designed also the street telephone kiosk, in its smallness and unadorned simplicity. All over the land today, multiplied many times, it can be seen and used. (In a great cathedral, people talk to God; in a street-side telephone kiosk, they talk to each other.)

But the beautiful balance can be seen by those who have eyes to see. Sir Giles's building symbolizes so clearly the values our Lord and Master spoke of so tellingly: 'He that is faithful in that which is *least*, is faithful also in *much*' (Luke 16:10, A.V.). Dr Moffatt's translation of His words is a little less familiar – and so, perhaps, more telling: 'He who is faithful with a *trifle*, is also faithful with *a large trust*.'

Many of us dream of doing great things – some actually do them – but not all of us balance this service of our lives, with the doing of 'small things'. Our Lord and Master talked about His followers offering in service 'a cup of cold water' in His Name. Nothing could be simpler – but with the right spirit, in that hot and thirsty land in which lived those who first heard His words, nothing could be more serviceable.

'The Christianity that conquered the Roman Empire', Dr T. W. Manson rejoices to remind us, 'was not an affair of brilliant preachers addressing packed congregations. We have, so far as I know, nothing much in the way of brilliant preachers in the first three hundred years of the Church's life. There were one or two brilliant conversationalists, but I suspect that they made more enemies than friends; and the greatest of them all, Origen, was probably over the head of most people most of the time. The great preachers came after Constantine the Great; but before that Christianity had already done its work and made its way right through the Empire from end to end.' 'How?' we might well ask. 'When we try to picture how it was done,' continues Dr Manson, 'we seem to see *domestic servants teaching Christ in and through their domestic service, workers doing it through their work, small shopkeepers through their trade, and so on*, rather than eloquent propagandists swaying mass meetings of interested enquirers.'

And it is so today – there is a call within the Eternal Kingdom for service '*both great and small*'. And those of us able to move about this world, with our eyes open and our spirits receptive, can find – as I find, in Sir Giles

Gilbert Scott's work – stirring reminders of this lovely balance.

From this great building, my thoughts go as helpfully to one of the *humblest* buildings I have ever entered – the little whitewashed home of that dear Irish Christian, Anna, 'My Lady of the Chimney Corner'. There her neighbours with joy or sorrow sought her out. She has 'gone upon her way' many years now; but many of us owe a debt to her son, with better opportunities than his humble father, Jamie the shoemaker, and his mother Anna ever knew. He wrote the story of those two loved people, and the little home in which they lived. All Antrim knew its way to that ever-open door. Anna daily whitewashed her hearthstone, and hung the kindly kettle on its hook, and stirred the peat fire. And to this day, I was able to discover, as I journeyed from Belfast to Portrush for a speaking engagement, the little whitewashed house stands, much as when their story was written true to life. I had some difficulty in seeking out a relative with a key to let me in, but a fine welcome awaited me when I did. All the simple personal belongings mentioned in the book are there, in much the order of Anna's lifetime, sitting in her chimney corner, just above the earthen floor. Jamie's barrel for soaking the leather is still there, alongside his workbench. And Anna's teacup remains – white with its blue pattern. It is all very simple, but that is its rightness to those of us who have been enriched in spirit by their minister son's story.

Above all, there remains in the memory of many of us, Anna's shining faith: 'God takes a han' wherever He can find it, an' just diz what He likes wi' it. Sometimes He takes a bishop's an' lays it on a child's head in benediction, then he takes the han' of a docther to relieve pain, th' han' of an aul' craither like me t' give a bit comfort to a neighbour.

But they're all han's touch't be His spirit, an' His Spirit is everywhere lukin' fur han's to use.'

So have I found buildings speaking to me – underlining 'both great and small' issues!

There Is Nothing Like It!

I can't think of anything more alive in God's earth than spring in the English countryside! Budding branches, green lawns and crocuses, even in the parks of great London, are wonderful – but to spend a few days away from its thundering traffic and haste is an experience to set one singing!

A living common, with its beech woods, slipped away behind me, as I drove my little car – and three verses of Eleanor Farjeon's 'A Morning Song', sang itself in my heart:

> Morning has broken
> Like the first morning,
> Blackbird has spoken
>   Like the first bird.
>   Praise for the singing!
>   Praise for the morning!
>   Praise for them, springing
>   From the First Word!
>
>
> Sweet the rain's new fall
> Sunlit from heaven,
> Like the first dewfall
>   On the first grass.
>   Praise for the sweetness
>   Of the wet garden,
>   Sprung in completeness
>   Where His feet pass!

Mine is the sunlight!
Mine is the morning
Born of the one light
   Eden saw play!
      Praise with elation,
      Praise every morning,
      God's re-creation
      Of the new day!

In a short time, I pulled up in the small village of Turville. The first person I saw was a woman on her knees, scrubbing a tombstone in the grass cemetery.

'Having a clean up?' I questioned her.

'Yes', said she. 'I've meant to do it for some time; and this morning seemed a good time to start.'

Then our talk moved from the tombstone to the village itself, set demurely about us on its green. Its church was flint-walled. The only sounds, beside the swish-swosh of her scrubbing brush in short strokes up and down, were the contented village sounds of hens laying, and nearer, in the trees, chirping birds.

'I suppose', I added, 'some, who don't know what goes on here, would call the village sleepy.'

'Yes,' came her answer, 'and some as knows what once went on here, wouldn't say much better.' And I heard the story of the woman who slept for seven years.

'Seven years!'

'Yes! My old mother-in-law – not long dead, at ninety-three – knew her well.' Then, holding her scrubbing brush idle a moment, she elaborated: 'While she was asleep, this village became quite famous. There used to be carriages drawn up all along the green – smart people from Henley, and doctors from London.'

'And did she really sleep for seven years?' I found myself asking.

'Well,' she answered me, pausing a moment more, 'they said she did, but I think her mother gave her something. They said the doctors examined her all over for pricks, in case a needle had been used. But I don't know. I always thought it queer that her mother wouldn't let any visitors go up the stairs to see her, not ahead of her. They do say', finished my new acquaintance, rising stiffly from her bucket and scrubbing brush, 'that from the churchyard at night, a shadow could be seen moving against the blind. But I don't know – they say she slept for seven years. The cottage where they lived is at the end there, where you came through the gate, and it's still called "The Sleepy House".'

'And what was the end of it?' I asked. 'Did she die?' (Though I couldn't think that she really lived, at the time.)

'No!' came the surprising answer. 'No, her mother died, and she got up!'

Since that spring day, when the world was full of Life, I've often wondered about little Turville, and its incredible story. And it jumps into my mind, whenever I hear anybody talk about Sin . . . even the greatest Sin. It's not my lot to know, or my business to judge, but I do feel that *to refuse Life is a very great Sin*! Our Lord said that He came to give men and women Life – and Life more abundant. This seems like throwing His gift in His face! (John 10:10, A.V.).

My friend, Dr William Barclay of Glasgow University, commented on this word of our Lord, in his little book on St John's gospel, in his *Daily Readings*: 'The phrase which is used for having Life more abundantly, is the Greek phrase which means to have *a surplus, a super-abundance of a thing, of Life*!'

Also in our time Herbert Butterfield – another fine, level-headed Christian, Professor of Modern History at Cambridge – said to those of us prepared to heed his words:

'*One of the greatest deficiencies of our time is the failure of the imagination or the intellect to bring home to itself the portentous character of human Sin.*' For this is what robs us of what Christ declared He came to bring us: *Life, Abundant Life, Eternal Life, in quality, not alone in quantity!*

One might well lay this charge against Turville's young woman who, prompted by her mother, turned her face against full Life for seven years' sleep. I wouldn't like to have to declare to you which is the greatest human Sin. It is not my business to judge – but I do feel that *to refuse Life is a very great Sin*!

Another fine university Christian of our time, Dr C. S. Lewis, says of us modern men and women, we are not just patients that the psychologist can take in hand – creatures of inhibitions and repressions – that a little clinical tinkering will put right: 'We are', he says, 'wilful, foolish, fallen men and women, who set up against the Great Giver of Life, refuse His Greatest Gift. We are [he makes very clear] not just creatures who need improvement, *but rebels who must lay down our arms.*'

And this is true, it is important to realize, right from the beginning, dealing with Life, as it comes to us. One must accept this gift in all its fulness, from the Lord of Life!

> Life is too brief
> Between the budding and the falling leaf,
> Between the seed-time and the golden sheaf,
> For hate and spite.
>
> Anon.

C. E. Montague, in his novel *Rough Justice*, introduces us to one who in life's springtime, accepts what he is offered. He tries to explain it to his father, but it's not easy

– it never is, to a member of one's family – though the youth speaks straightly: 'There's Christ. I do believe, sir, I've loved Him – of course, it's a big word to use, but I've really loved every manjack thing about Him ever since I first heard of His death, and hid in the rhododendrons to blub. *Whatever He said seems to grow into a bit of yourself*, till you can't make up your mind what to do, in anything big, without thinking first, "If I should do this, would Christ bar me?"'

He is talking of Life – 'and Life more abundant' – and of his own early choice. There's nothing like it!

Chains Can Hinder

It was a peaceful, sun-flecked summer morning that brought me to Wimborne Minster, in the south of England. For centuries before, other lovers of reading had come that way. Most had been wholly dependent on what the Minster's chained-library of more than two hundred books could offer.

Among those rich treasures was a Breeches Bible. It got its name, of course, from its quaint rendering of a verse where it says that Adam and Eve 'sewed fig-leaves together and made themselves breeches'. Today, more of us are able to read – and we have our own Bibles. Happily, we have no need to walk dusty miles to the Minster to avail ourselves of what it can offer through a *chained-book*. At one time, books were so precious and so rare, that it was an accepted thing to chain them to constant places of reading.

If, in the early centuries, it was sensible to ask: 'What do Christians read?' it must have been very early. 'At the time when the Church was born,' says Dr A. M. Chirgwin, 'no one expected it would produce a book which would come to occupy a central place in its life. The Founder of the Faith – our Lord and Master – neither wrote anything Himself, nor encouraged His disciples to write. He sent them out to preach and teach, and to bear witness of that which they had seen and heard, and all the evidence goes to show that they did it by word of mouth.

'Yet in spite of that, a book came into existence [partner, in Time, to the Old Testament] and came to be an indispensable element in the Church's life.'

If you ask me how it happened, I can only say that as far as the New Testament was concerned, the idea was to get the witness and words of Jesus down into writing, whilst those who heard them, and saw aspects of His ministry, were still living. Then, too, there was the possibility that with the passage of time, the transforming Message might be forgotten or corrupted, if left to men's memories. A third factor was the persistent journeyings of the early Christians. They seemed possessed of a divine restlessness – they wanted men and women in every part of the known world of their day to share the shining reality of their Faith. Dr Chirgwin begins at that point to give us a bird's-eye view of that ever-enlarging enterprise. 'Peter', he reminds us, 'went to Caesarea and Joppa; Philip went to Samaria and the South Country; Paul and Barnabas went to Antioch and from there started on their great missionary journeys that took one or both of them over much of Western Asia and Southern Europe; Priscilla and Acquila went from Rome to Corinth; Timothy from Rome to Ephesus; Luke from Troas to Athens; Apollos from Alexandria to Rome. They criss-crossed the world of their time.'

There were any number of converts and communities that, with the passing of Time, could not have an Apostle always in their midst – but they could receive letters, like the letters of St Paul which occupy a large part of the New Testament. These kept them close to essential Christian truth; and, added to that point of tremendous importance, enabled them to have something dependable to share. How else could these disciples – men and women, both – hand on their Faith with certainty? How be as sure of it, when their memories began to fade with age?

The helpful, heart-stirring place that the Book came to have in their lives, is understandable. Tertullian, the early Christian theologian (160–230), from the start of his faith with joy unflagging declared that *the Bible was for everyone*. Not all could read; but this stout-heart for things Christian used it constantly when involved in dealing with the heresies that arose from time to time in the early days of the Church. And gradually those who heard him came also to acknowledge the authority of the Book. And other great leaders underlined his conviction: 'I cannot sufficiently urge you to devote yourself to the reading of the Bible', said Jerome, to one he cared for. Chrysostom, one of the great fathers of the Church (345–407), said in his turn: 'Every Christian should buy one, and should never part with it.'

And through the long centuries, there has never been any doubt on this point, not least, when it came into our language. The old Breeches Bible of 1560 early appeared in churches, cathedrals and minsters *chained* to the set reading place, due to the scarcity of books. The most widely used version of my lifetime has been the Authorized or King James's Version of 1611; and by general acclaim it is a glorious possession: 'The best words of the best period of English in the best order.' It never fails to delight the cultivated lover of our language. Its lovely phrases linger in the memory – especially, perhaps, those to be found in the Psalms, where beauty and truth are imperishably enshrined in such phrases as 'the strength of the hills', 'the wings of the morning', 'mine own familiar friend', 'we spend our years as a tale that is told', 'the valley of the shadow of Death'.

But again and again, for all its beauty, the same Authorized Version is for many chained to a form of expression long outmoded. More than three hundred words have changed their meaning since 1611 – words like 'ghost' for 'spirit', 'quick' for 'alive'; we know what we mean by 'quick', but when we come upon it in our Bible reading, the lovely, on-going, liberating truth is 'chained' for any practical purposes in our daily life.

'Comfort' is another word that has completely changed. It appears in its old English sense of *strengthening*, a number of times; the best-known one is perhaps that of the twenty-third psalm: 'Thy rod and Thy staff they comfort me.' The word, as commonly understood when the Authorized Version came out, had nothing to do with the ease of the armchair, or a smooth pillow, or soothing words.

And so it is with the Bible word 'conversation', as found in Psalm 37:14, and Psalm 50:23, A.V. It is not a casual pleasance of the street, church porch, garden gate – not a matter of words at all. It means, in the early sense, general behaviour or conduct.

Another early English word used in the Authorized Version of the Bible which unhappily 'chains' the living truth, is 'prevent'. We know what we mean by it; but in its original sense it has to do with one who goes before his master on a journey, to make ready his reception and lodging place. It is a word we get in the beautiful old English collect: 'Prevent us, O Lord, in all our doings with Thy most gracious favour.' (It is the very opposite of hinder, or stop altogether.) Hugh Redwood, a widely known London journalist, tells in his autobiography, *Bristol Fashion*, how he happened on a pencilled translation of this word, in the margin of a Bible in a home where he was a guest. It read: 'My God in His loving kindness shall meet me at every corner.'

It is plain that we must welcome one of the modern translations of the Bible, if we are to 'unchain' its glorious truth, and make it today available to all men and women, as it was always intended that it should be. It must be free to carry true meaning into the inmost secret places of their lives. Canon J. B. Phillips, Bible translator, says: 'I felt, and feel, without any shadow of doubt, that close contact with the gospels builds up in the heart and mind a character of awe-inspiring stature and quality. I have read, in Greek and Latin, scores of myths, but I did not feel the slightest flavour of myth here. There is an almost childlike candour and simplicity, and *the total effect is tremendous*.'

At no time in history have people been so well served with scholarly, readable translations, so easily available!

Needed Encouragement

It is a joy to be a gardener. But, however little experienced, you will discover that soil is not all, though it can be discouraging.

For sixteen years, my home-sharing friend and I gardened on the top of a yellow clay hill, at our beloved 'West Hills'. Many efforts, seed-packets, cuttings, young shrubs, and lively hopes were ours.

And whenever we had time to spare, I got out the little car, two shovels and a sack or two, and we made off down to a nearby beach for seaweed, the equivalent in bulk of two passengers. And when finally dug in, it got a welcome from our stubborn yellow soil.

After some time, we learned of an old sawmill site, a way off in the other direction, and out came the sacks once more. I sought out a long-retired mill boss, and he expressed himself pleased to let us explore there. Our effort resulted in a pile of soft, black, decayed sawdust, and soon we were dumping that on top of our seaweed-covered patch.

Nor was that all. Months rolled by, and Rene's birthday came. Friends were kind, and two arrived one evening with their special gift, but, they had to explain, they couldn't bring it indoors. Our noses soon told us why. Our friend Geoff was a chicken farmer – and he was quick to say that their gift, two sacks of manure, was for our garden.

This trilogy of seaweed, sawdust, and chicken-manure – repeated season after season – in time had our soil soft and black. But it meant a great deal of effort. Nor was hard, yellow clay our only discouragement – *there were birds*!

Our Master, long ago, took notice of things of Nature, as He trod the country footpaths. And what He shared of observation lives on to this day, within the parables of the New Testament. In one He told how 'a sower went forth to sow' – and I know his hopeful expectations (Matthew 13:3, R.S.V.). 'As he sowed, some seeds fell along the path [very hard and unproductive!] and the birds came and devoured them.' That discouragement is all too widespread.

In the little land where Jesus spent His earthly life, it was especially so. Fortunately, *some* of the seeds 'fell on *good* soil, and brought forth – some an hundred-fold, some sixty, some only thirty.' And those of us who are servants of the soil are likely to remember this. That soil to this day – as those of us who have walked in little Palestine know – is more stubborn than in most places on the earth's surface. And there never was a closer observer than our Master, constantly moving about from village to village, speaking and ministering to the needs of the people. Nothing escaped Him. His New Testament parables remind us of that, as T. T. Lynch would have us remember:

> He spoke of grass and wind and rain,
> And fig-trees and fine weather;
> And made it His delight to bring
> Heaven and earth together.
>
> He spoke of lilies, corn and vines,
> *The sparrow and the raven*;
> And words so natural, and yet so wise
> Were on men's hearts engraven.
>
> Anon.

But when one had sown well, and known reasonable hope, there was still the hazard of the birds. In Palestine, one authority tells us, were some three hundred species, twenty-six of them unique. Added to established breeds were those which came year by year. Little Palestine offered a long-established bird migration path. 'The narrow land-bridge connecting African Egypt', we are told, 'with the hinterlands of Asia Minor and the valleys of Mesopotamia have been used since pre-historic times.'

No wonder our Master spoke warningly of *the birds* – not only of the familiars, but of the occasional migratories. What damage they could do! What discouragement inflict!

This dawned upon me afresh, as a gardener, when moving open-eyed in St Paul's Cathedral in London. (The service over, it was good to ponder on the inscriptions there to honour good men and women – who, on this earth on which we find ourselves, had found some inner secrets of achievement.) One of them, serving the Kingdom of Christ in the East End of London, and greatly loved during that time, was Canon Barnett. I shall never forget now his memorial tablet in St Paul's, and the encouragement that its words speak daily, as if directly from our Master – a message that supports the servant of His Spirit in any part of the earth: '*Fear not to sow because of the birds!*'

Canon Barnett, in our day, was one of Christ's good sowers of Christian truth here on earth. All that he sowed did not come to fruition. *He might well have given up – but he didn't.*

And now his memorial tablet is an encouragement to you and me: 'Fear not to sow because of the birds!'

They all too easily represent discouragement at many levels of life. Dr J. Alan Kay, my editor, and I once talked about this in his London office. And later, in his published sermons *The Wise Design*, I found an enlargement of the same theme: 'He who would live successfully, and particularly he who would live as a Christian successfully, must learn the lesson of persistence.

'One of the people we must learn to persist with', he continues, 'is ourselves. *We easily get discouraged*; we fail and lose heart, and doubt our ability, and relax our effort. I think it would help us in that if we could grasp the fact that we cannot expect to do God's work perfectly in five minutes or five years, or fifty. It is in the very nature of things that we should not be perfect and do everything well from the very first moment that we start the Christian life. The world is made like that, and so are we.

'After all, the work of God on which we are engaged is one requiring very considerable skill, and skill is not automatic; it is only attained by persistent work. Skill at any work that is worthwhile does not come of itself; it needs practice day after day and week after week and year after year. We as Christians are supposed to be skilled in loving. And skill in loving is like any other skill in that it is not come by without thought. We begin by loving clumsily – both God and our neighbour; we do the wrong things, we make mistakes. If we would ever learn to do it perfectly, we must persist.'

And to that end, we need all the encouragement we can give, and receive. We must let nothing that we encounter in this life discourage us – *not even the birds!*

On My Two Feet!

My friend Rene and I had been on the road in southern England for many days, when we heard of Saint Cross, the oldest almshouse in all England. And we were glad that we did. We decided to walk on beyond glorious Winchester Cathedral, where we had been some time.

In the year 1136 the Hospital of Saint Cross had been founded to 'shelter thirteen poor men – and to give food and drink to poor wayfarers who came to its gates'.

At the porter's hatchway, we caught up with another tired traveller. He had asked for the Wayfarer's Dole – a horn vessel of ale and a piece of bread. Soon, we in turn stood before the hatchway, expecting to be served. But the old porter said: 'We never offer the Wayfarer's Dole – you have to ask for it.' So one by one, we asked for and were given the ancient symbol of compassion.

Since then, the old porter's injunction has recalled to me the Master's '*Ask*, and it shall be given you; *seek*, and ye shall find; *knock*, and it shall be opened to you.' Asking, seeking and knocking are, one grasps as one advances in Christian living, *secrets of petitionary prayer*.

At first, aware of the greatness and loving concern of God, one is liable to leave the whole matter to Him. 'He is so wise', we say, 'He will know better than any one of us earth-dwellers what we need – why ask Him?'

But, as at Saint Cross, always there are two parties involved in the very deep things in life: hunger, thirst, fellowship. We are not there *begging*, when we ask, seek and knock; much less, are we *coercing* an unwilling God. *We are revealing our eagerness to receive a gracious gift.*

60

That it was sometimes lacking was a painful discovery that Jesus, in His turn, had to make here in His earth-life. He does not tell us of it in detail, but He does say of those with whom He had such dealings: '*How often would I . . . and ye would not!*' And it happened within the very city He loved of all cities on earth; and amongst religious men and women, with the longest training, who might have been thought to know better. There is no missing the loneliness of that relationship, and the failure of it: 'O Jerusalem, Jerusalem, thou that killest the prophets, and stonest them that are sent unto thee, how often would I have gathered thy children together, even as a hen gathereth her chickens under her wing, *and ye would not*!' (Matthew 23:37, A.V.).

In his revealing words, the beloved Archbishop Trench said in a time nearer to us: 'We must not conceive of prayer as an overcoming of God's reluctance, but as a laying hold of His highest willingness.'

Another fallacy underlying the belief that the wisdom and love of God makes petitionary prayer superfluous, is a like idea – a mistaken idea – that God can not only decide, but do things without help from us. Dr Harry Fosdick thinks about this, and surely he is right: 'God Himself', he says, 'cannot do some things *unless we think*. He never blazons His truth on the sky that men may find it without seeking. Only when men gird the loins of their minds, and undiscourageably give themselves to intellectual toil, will God reveal to them the truth, even about the physical world. And God Himself cannot do some things unless men *work*. Will a man say that when God wants bridges and tunnels, wants the lightnings harnessed, and cathedrals built, He will do the work Himself? That is absurd . . . God stores the hills with marble, but he never built a Parthenon: He fills the mountains with ore, but He never made a needle, nor a locomotive . . . *Now, if God has left some things contingent on our thinking, and on our working, why may He not have left some things contingent on our praying?'*

I feel sure that He has – so much hinges on petitionary prayer: our asking, seeking, knocking. The threefold secret, I am now a long time persuaded, is not resignation to God's solitary Will; but the offering of our words, with our warmest, realest *co-operation*, our fullest purpose and power.

Marianne Farningham may not be known to us all, but she sums up this reality in a little prayer – and what a world-moving prayer:

> In the glad morning of my day,
> My life to give, my vows to pay,
> With no reserve, and no delay,
> *With all my heart, I come!*

With that spirit breaking through, God can work wonders. He can do things that He wants to do – but for which He needs the co-operation of the loving, giving members of His earth-family, not least the receiving members. So one by one, as we grasp the secret of this spiritual reality, let us each 'ask', 'seek', and 'knock'. With eagerness, then, we declare ourselves sons and daughters, co-workers in God's eternal purpose.

For long on a city's 'slummy side', He had cherished a dream, when first I walked in Chicago. By then, Jane Addams had come upon the scene, and I made time in a busy, strenuous visit to walk down a part that both she and God knew well.

There had been a time when garbage cans stood there, inviting alley rats and miserable slum-sicknesses. Then Jane and her enterprising colleagues moved into 'T' old Hull House'. It was extraordinarily shabby, with some of its space having been taken over for storing factory furniture; but it did not long stay that way, because God's will had got across to Jane's stout heart. Before long, others of the city who had been praying in desperate eagerness for God to do something, found that He was! He and Jane together!

And the lonely, the cheerless, the purposeless, the poor, found their way to that old house, that somebody now called by a new name: *la Casa di Dio* – 'The House of God'. To their amazement, they heard wholesome laughter ringing out there, and saw wonderful adventures of mind and spirit grow, long before Jane, as Head, had been granted a half-share in the Nobel Peace Prize. That was a moment of rejoicing! People of all nationalities gladly gathered there to share life! 'You inhabit reality', William James had said to Jane – and she did. She knew how to ask, to seek, and to knock – to throw her whole gladsome being, body, mind and spirit, into the business, with God!

Thanks to two jaunts on my two feet – to Saint Cross, and through a poor area of Chicago – my prayer-life now carries more meaning!

Wake Up and Dream

Children are funny sometimes, but often with a meaningful freshness, until we adults laugh it out of them. And that's a pity! Elizabeth Taylor, who has given us a number of novels of English life, shares one charming example. 'I remember', says she, 'going one morning to wake up my daughter when she was very small. She opened her eyes, and said: "Put your head down on the pillow, and get the rest of my lovely dream."'

It was, of course, a night-time dream. But none of us can get far without a '*day-time dream*'. That has been expressed before, it's not, by any means, original. Actually, I came upon a striking poster, bearing but four words, as I hurried along a familiar street a while ago, thinking of something different. And I've set its four words at the head of this chapter: '*Wake up, and dream!*'

Our world-life is very much richer, I believe, because here and there men and women have risen to that challenge. I used to think that to be pointed out as a dreamer was to be involved in some kind of shameful activity – but no longer. I blame that on an early story-teller and her narration of young Joseph and his brothers, who clubbed together against him. The early Genesis account of this (Genesis 37:3–5, A.V.) says: 'Joseph, being seventeen years old, was feeding the flock with his brethren; and the lad was with the sons of Bilhah, and with the sons of Zilpah . . . and Joseph brought unto his father their evil report. Now Israel loved Joseph more than all his children, because he was the son of his old age: and he made him a coat of many colours.'

Night after night, young Joseph dreamed, and during the days following, told some of his dreams to his brothers. Far from being interested, as he felt sure they would be, they spoke against him the more. Some time later, they set off for Dothan; 'and Joseph', the old record says, 'went after his brethren, and found them in Dothan. And when they saw him afar off, even before he came near unto them, they conspired against him to slay him. And they said one to another, "*Behold, this dreamer cometh*".'

Looking back on that happening from our day, the commentator of *The Interpreter's Bible* says at once: 'If they had been men of more magnanimous spirit, they would have thought and felt differently. If they could not share Jacob's fondness for their young brother, they would have treated his dreaming with amusement . . . Joseph could have done them good. They were the sort of men who did not really think or do anything different – commonplace men who, left to themselves, will keep everything around them commonplace. But the fact that Joseph was around, meant that they could not be left to themselves.'

Young Joseph's dreams, of course, were night-time dreams – not so practical as a day-time dream can be!

To disregard, not to mention ridicule, another's dreams is a sin against one's fellows – but how often it happens. Freya Stark, in her striking book *Perseus in the Wind*, says: 'I often think of this when I see a defeated face in some small orchestra, that grinds empty tunes among laughter and scraping of chairs and clink of tables in a place where music is forgotten; and I try to read, under the dull routine and set crust of features, *what dreams first ushered in the morning to that fat opaque man blowing his trombone, or to the nervous youth with shabby eyes who rests his violin so wearily upon his knee when the piece is finished, and turns the page of his music with such dead hands.*

'They must have started out with visions of obedient orchestras and lamplit applause; and listened to Ariel voices in the gossip of the air; until contact not with the real, but with the bitter world of men, and their own weakly furnished spirits, flung them like economic driftwood on a bare shore.'

But it's not only our relationship with dreamers that I'm concerned about, it's the challenge to be a dreamer myself, implicit in our title.

One of the most wonderful days, on all my world journeys, was spent in Zerka, a long car drive from Jerusalem. For there I met 'a dreamer'! One of Christ's Dreamers: Miss Winifred Coate, a silvery-haired teacher, at the close of thirty-nine years' service to young folk, an Anglican Christian.

She lived in Zerka, formerly a burnt-up, trackless wilderness of sand and stones. At one time, centuries past, Crusader buildings had stood thereabouts, under the wide sky. But these had sunk out of sight, and almost out of memory. It was all a matter of the searing heat of the sun, and an absence of water. Though within a reasonable distance of Amman, the capital, there was no life there – not a blade of grass, not a living creature even of the lowliest kind, save perhaps an occasional *jerboa*, a desert rat that passing Bedouin travellers might catch and eat. The centuries-old hindrance was lack of water. There was no water, everybody knew – everybody, that is, but the silvery-haired English woman, Winifred Coate. She dreamed of doing something with these wasting acres, and acquired many of them; she dreamed of cultivating and growing things, of helping the Arab refugees she saw looking wistfully at what each day brought. She argued that if, long ago, people had lived there, surely there had been water then – and who could say that there was no water at the present? On the arid surface, as far as the eye could see, there was certainly nothing to argue the possibility. But that did not deter Christ's Dreamer – though when she passed amongst them, men shook their heads and spoke of her undertaking as 'Coate's Folly'.

She addressed her need for help to the Save the Children Fund, for aid in erecting the first simple homes, if water could be found. In their reply, they underlined the word '*If*' – for it all depended, they knew, on water being to hand. There was no point in pretending: life and water were linked!

So Winifred Coate engaged one Abu Nakhleh, a water-diviner, armed with a simple piece of twig, to walk patiently up and down over that pitiful piece of the earth's surface. Time passed! And there was, alas, nothing to report. Four other men were engaged to undertake other necessary tasks – to pick up stones and shovel them away; to clear areas under the savagely hot sun; to mark out roads, and build dry walls. A tiny building was raised in time, with money forthcoming from Christian Aid, to be a shelter for the workers by day, and for the two watchmen keeping guard over their few tools by night.

It was slow work, and hard. Then one day, quite suddenly, Abu Nakhleh's little twig resisted. *There was water there!* Others were brought in to make a thorough test – but how much water was there, was still the question, and how far down? At any rate Oxfam, receiving the exciting news, was prepared to help. And in no time desert people – who were nobody's care – came flocking to see a miracle they had only heard about: pure, sweet water gushing up out of the ground!

There were no sneers now – the old teacher's dream was coming true! Under guidance, other wells were dug, irrigation channels appeared; and again, under guidance, fathers of families long dispirited began to plant, to plant, to plant! Simple houses went up, and the first needy families moved in.

In an astonishingly short time, they had fresh food to eat – lentils, cucumbers, lettuce, celery, peppers – and to sell to the distant market. In due time, lush clover and alfalfa began to cover the naked earth. King Hussein paid the infant settlement a visit, and gave it the name Abdelliyeh. The news got abroad; and the Government made a gift to it of many additional acres of desert.

A dream? Yes! Led by a very practical dreamer – as day-time dreamers often are! The wonderful day I walked about there, lunching with Miss Coate, and talking over her experience to date, little children played about their small white homes, their fathers busy with tilling, or pottery, or with the breeding and tending of a dairy-herd, their mothers preparing more nourishing meals than they'd known for a long time!

A dream! A day-time dream – and so practical!

Jesus cherished a dream just as practical – He called it 'the Kingdom of God'. He began His ministry with the declaration: 'The Kingdom . . . is at hand!' 'Jesus came into Galilee', says Matthew (4:23, A.V.), 'preaching the *Gospel of the Kingdom of God.*' He sent out His twelve disciples with almost the same words – certainly with the same dream – and later the Seventy; and His last teaching before His ascension carried the same emphasis: 'Being seen of them forty days, and *speaking of the things pertaining to the Kingdom of God.*' The words were always on His lips, the dream always in His heart!

And today, every time we pray the Lord's Prayer, we pray, 'Thy Kingdom come . . .', identifying ourselves with that dream of His! Considering the kind of world we live in, which supplies the doings we read of in our newspapers, it seems a daring thing to grasp that dream. *But we must!* My old editor, Dr Leslie Church, once offered me a good lead: *I shall not surrender my Dream. When I am tempted, I shall kneel and say, "Our Father . . . Thy Kingdom come" – and kneeling, I will break down the last barrier in my heart!'*

Did Jesus Ever Laugh?

Bright young Frances, still in her college uniform, sat at a little table in the window. Pencil and New Testament poised, she had just returned from the Wednesday Scripture class, after college, carrying her question with her: 'Did Jesus ever laugh?'

No one had ever put that question to me before. After a moment's pause, I recalled one or two New Testament passages, and fashioned my answer. Those passages were impressive against the dispiriting solemnity of many Bible pictures – or what some churches called 'holy pictures'. He is there shown weeping over the City that refused Him, or hanging on the Cross. (Of course, He was described as 'the Man of Sorrows, and acquainted with grief', and He certainly was, and one had to step reverently for that reason. No one ever suffered sorrow like unto His sorrow – but I dare to believe that no one knew deep down laughter, like His.)

He drew little children to Himself, and that was one proof to young Frances and me, as we talked about Him. He was received in the villages and homes as a great religious leader, but not as other religious leaders.

In the East there was a saying, as recorded in the Apocrypha, 'The fool lifts up his voice in laughter, but the wise man will scarcely smile quietly.' But it is plain that Jesus was different, as the types of laughter amongst men and women are different. There is the laughter that in his time, nearer our own, the old philosopher Thomas Hobbes called 'A sudden glory'. It was as if on an overclouded scene the sun suddenly came out. And what a joy that was!

I think that was often the kind of laughter Jesus knew – bringing a new spirit to a discouraging situation, winning the affection and shining trust of little children among others. Dr Alec Vidler, in his study of Mark's gospel – where this happy relationship between Jesus and the children is recorded – says, 'The word Mark uses can mean children of up to twelve years of age.' The disciples did all they could to discourage this, 'but when Jesus saw it', says our Authorized New Testament (Mark 10:14), 'He was much displeased, and said unto them, "Suffer the little children to come unto Me, and forbid them not: for of such is the kingdom of God. Verily I say unto you, whosoever shall not receive the kingdom of God as a little child, he shall not enter therein." And He took them up in His arms, and put His hands upon them and blessed them.'

And there are other occasions of the most natural adult relationship recorded in the New Testament. Jesus spent a lot of time with his men disciples, travelling, eating and sleeping. Sometimes they were overcrowded, at other times relaxed as the day came to a close. Good healthy men – you can't tell me that laughter did not sometimes envelop their company, led sometimes by their Master Who had been a craftsman!

He took them away with Him sometimes to rest awhile in a quiet country spot. He surely led them in laughter there, He was such a healthy and well-balanced Man all the time. One of His strong-limbed, level-hearted modern followers was Thomas Kelly, the American college man, of whom someone wrote: 'I cannot tell you adequately, and yet I think you know, how much I loved Tom. He was my great friend and comrade here; there was no one else who entered the inner circle of the heart, or shared the heights of the soul. He was the perfect friend, whether we shared the gay sunlight of humour, or ascended the peaks of highest vision together . . . He was a man – a whole man of body, mind and spirit, like his Master!' Another wrote of him: 'There was a natural attractiveness and lovableness about Thomas Kelly that drew students and colleagues to him . . . He *laughed* with the rich heart abandon of wind and sun . . . I never heard richer, heartier laughter than his. He delighted in earth's incongruities, all the more perhaps because he saw eternal things and the values that transcend the earth . . . even the publicans and sinners among the students respected and loved him; he said to all . . . "Not till the sun refuses you do I refuse you".' One feels he was like his Master, Jesus, Man-and-God, and many found inspiration in him.

To such men and women on this earth of God's, we owe a great deal; for laughter – in all its glory – was first God's idea. If it didn't come from Him, where indeed did it come from?

Jesus was the Perfect Man, and God would never have expected Him to live a balanced life on this earth of ours, with its ups and downs, without true laughter. (In this, we see things differently from the writer in the Apocrypha, and others round about him.) As things were, critics found John the Baptist, Jesus's forerunner, too solemn, and Jesus too happy. Jesus was so gloriously balanced, He saw not only the children in the streets who played funerals; He saw also those who took out their little pipes, and played weddings! (Matthew 11:16, A.V.).

Jesus delighted to compare His companionship with His followers as being like a continual wedding feast (Mark 2:19, A.V.). You can't imagine a Man, thinking of things like this, to be a Man Who continually looked at life solemnly. That would be unbalanced, and impossible! There is no forgetting that when He set out upon His public ministry, his first public gathering was at a wedding feast, where He was a welcome guest. Would anyone ever be invited to a wedding feast if he was known to be so solemn that he never laughed? (John 2:1, A.V.).

The one care a Christian should add to his laughter, of course, is kindliness. It is recorded in one place in the gospels, that those present where Jesus was, 'laughed Him to scorn'. He had gone into the home of Jairus to offer help to a little daughter. It was a house full of grief – and where laughter would have been completely out of place, not least the laughter of scorn. Jesus laughed *with* people not *at* people (Matthew 9:24, A.V.).

When we come to examine the stories Jesus told, we find Him one of the sunniest teachers in all history. 'He loved playful exaggeration, or what we call the grotesque', says Professor J. A. Findlay. 'Ye strain at a gnat', He says, 'and swallow a camel.' Then Findlay goes on to sum up: 'No one can even try to imagine a man swallowing a camel without inward laughter . . .

'There is another kind of story,' says the Professor, 'for laughter and tears are never far apart in the teaching of Jesus. We think of the extraordinarily effective tale of the rich fool' (Luke 12:16–21, A.V.).

Another of His stories concerns three guests invited to a grand feast, and the excuses they give for not coming – the last, *the most laughable of all*: 'I have married a wife, and therefore I cannot come!' (Luke 14:18–20, A.V.).

Laughter is a great part in the winsomeness of any man or woman we admire. And I can't think that Jesus is any exception.

The Sunnier Side of Doubt

I have to thank the poet Tennyson for this title; it comes from his lines:

> *Cleave to the sunnier side of doubt,*
> And cling to Faith beyond the forms of Faith.

Doubt, to most of us, carries a suggestion of darkness, diffidence and discouragement; but behind his words is a new reality, and I take pleasure in sharing it. It may surprise you to learn that the very first sculpture I set out to find in the great city of Florence was that of the disciple we call 'Doubting Thomas'. Of all the Twelve chosen by our Lord, you might well dismiss Thomas as unattractive and unhelpful; but that, I have discovered in my on-going Christian life, would be a mistake. In Florence, a city full of lovely, meaningful sculpture, Verrocchio's figure of Doubting Thomas, under the title 'The Incredulity of St Thomas', has stayed in my memory to this hour. On the façades of Or San Michele, the Church of the Guilds, are niches holding figures of the patron saints of the Guilds, among them some of the finest fifteenth-century work the city has to rejoice in: Ghiberti's 'St John', 'St Matthew', 'St Stephen', and Verrocchio's 'The Incredulity of St Thomas'. And this last one I put first. It portrays the loving patience of our Risen Lord in revealing the mark of His sword-thrust to 'Doubting Thomas'. (You remember the setting: Thomas was not with his colleagues, the other disciples, when the Risen Master returned, speaking to them words of peace. Where he was, nobody knows; but

74

it makes it easier to understand Thomas's dilemma, and to understand, to our own encouragement, what our attractive title means: 'The sunnier side of doubt'.)

Dr James Hastings defines doubt as 'the growing-pain of the soul', and that underlines the fact that it need not be permanent, however painful while it lasts. Growing-pains belong to the youthful experience of growth, and in the sense in which Thomas knew doubt, to the growing-pain of Christian discipleship. Those of us who have discovered this in our own experience, can be helped by Thomas to 'the sunnier side of doubt'.

'Popular proverbial language', says our trusted Dr William Barclay, 'has dealt unkindly with Thomas, for Thomas is commemorated in the phrase "a doubting Thomas". No doubt there is an element of truth in that phrase, but there is also something very like a slander.'

Thomas was not the only disciple who found it difficult to believe in the Risen Christ – the first report to reach them had been dismissed *by all the disciples*. It was too big a claim to find lodging in their sorrowful, finite minds. When Mary ran back from the Open Tomb on the first Easter morning, with her news that the Tomb was empty, Peter, and that other disciple whom Jesus loved, John, couldn't believe it. 'And they ran both together' to the Tomb to see how things were (John 20:1–10, A.V.).

But Mary, with her tears, thinking that somebody had stolen away His body, stayed. 'The kind of emotional, unreasonable thing a woman would do', the men might have said when they knew where she was – as men go on saying of women's unexpected actions to this day. *But it was worth it.* For she met there with two angels who sat 'one at the head, and the other at the feet, where the body of Jesus had lain' (John 20:12, A.V.). 'And they said unto her, "Woman, why weepest thou?" She said unto them, "Because they have taken away my Lord, and I know not

where they have laid him!"' And at that point a wonder
awaited: a man, whom she took to be the gardener, spoke
to her: 'Woman, why weepest thou? Whom seekest thou?'
She said unto him, 'Sir, if thou hast borne him hence, tell
me where thou hast laid him, and I will take him away.'
(She fully believed, at that stage, that she was dealing with
the body of her crucified Master – certainly not with a
Living Lord.)

Then 'Jesus saith unto her, "*Mary!*" She turned herself,
and saith unto him, "*Rabboni!*"; which is to say, "*Master!*"
. . . Then Mary came and told the disciples that she had
seen the Lord, and that he had spoken these things unto
her' (John 20:13–18).

Thomas stands out, in any reference to him in the
gospels, as a straightforward man, anxious to know what
could reasonably be known in any event affecting him.
When his colleagues told him the amazing news – when he
returned after being away – that Jesus was alive, he did not
say the equivalent of 'Nonsense!' He said, in a very
common-sense way, 'Except I shall see in His hands, the
print of the nails, and put my finger into the print of the
nails, and thrust my hand into His side, I will not believe.'
*And the wonderful truth for us, is that Jesus met him at the
point of his doubt.* He did not chastise him; He said: 'Reach
hither thy finger, and behold My hands', when He returned
a second time, and Thomas was there, 'and reach hither thy
hand, and thrust it into My side: and be not faithless, but
believing.' In no time the most wonderful words Thomas
could summon, were on his lips: '*My Lord and my God!*'

And this is where you and I find the deep-down answer
to our doubts, in the presence of the Risen Christ. No
further this very moment from any one of us, than He was
then from Thomas; no less real because unseen! Take time
to turn over the gospel account of Thomas's experience,
especially that word that Jesus spoke then, that seems to

be addressed to all the rest of us: 'Thomas, because thou hast seen Me, thou hast believed: *blessed are they that have not seen, and yet have believed*' (John 20:26–29).

I don't for a minute think that *every* question that ever crossed Thomas's mind was suddenly answered – experience is against it – but in that moment, one great certainty gripped and held his life: *Christ was alive!* He had not merely survived Death – He had conquered it!

To doubt is not to sin, if it leads one to lay hold of Truth. Jesus never discouraged any doubter. To those who asked Him, early on: 'Where dwellest Thou?' His answer was, 'Come and see!' And to Thomas's word: 'Except I shall see . . . and thrust my hand into His side, I will not believe', His answer was as straightforward, and compassionate. That way, He enabled Thomas to come to the point where he could exclaim with wonder and joy: '*My Lord and my God!*'

And in our world today we need a similar experience: not an argument, but Himself! This way, we have every hope of coming through to 'the sunnier side of doubt'!

No Longer Lonely

A love letter is a private missive, but one fell into my hands lately. The young man who wrote it could never have guessed that this would happen. 'Far away from where I am now,' he wrote very charmingly, 'there is a little gap in the hills, and beyond it is the sea, and it is there I do be looking the whole day long, for 'tis the nearest thing to yourself that I can see.'

There is no doubt about his loneliness – if you are a normal human being, you will have some time experienced it yourself. And you don't have to be in love for that.

Aloneness and *loneliness*, of course, are not the same; though some confuse them. It is hard for some of us to be enough alone, especially in city life. Therein, loneliness can be one of the most painful realities. It knows no geography, it knows no class – the rich as well as the poor, and those of us in between can fall to it. It is even possible to be subject to loneliness in one's own home, if it lacks harmony, though, God be thanked, I have never known it there. But I have felt it, amidst workmates, and in the milling crowd. And, of course, there are isolated places like the island of Eigg, where it is often present in a very special sense. Kevin Crossly-Holland, in his book *Pieces of Land* (Gollancz) speaks of it: 'Most of Eigg', he says, 'consists of desolate moorland, covered with heather and bracken, punctuated with eyes of water that constantly change with the changing sky. Unless you have all day to follow string-thin sheepruns and the courses of burns across the plateau, to circumnavigate peat-bogs and outcrops of rock . . . Eigg has a long history', he adds, 'back

78

to early Irish martyrologies in connection with St Donnan, Brown Donnan of Eigg and Uist.' An interesting place in which to spend a few hours whilst on holiday, as an old woman said to Kevin Crossly-Holland. 'It's well for the visitor. But when you live here, when you're *old and lonely*, and there's no soul on the hills . . .' Her voice ceased at that point, but there was no need to say more.

Loneliness is no new experience, of course; but in the last few years it seems to have greatly increased in our Western world. Women seem especially vulnerable; when family life is finished and long hours lack accustomed interests, boredom is the first step to loneliness, and in this age, the life-span is so much greater than was once the case. Loneliness can seem worse in the light of the hasty lives of near relatives; and when long-time neighbours and friends are moved by house clearance schemes, when high-rise settlements go up. A tendency to brood over the past, is another contributory factor in loneliness, as is shyness. An absence of religious experience is worst of all, being outside the warmth of friendly human beings in the day-to-day fellowship of the Church. This comes on Sunday, but especially, perhaps, in small weekday gatherings, where there can be the give-and-take of interests, friendly talk, and common service.

The difficulty with loneliness is that people who never suffer it are often so uninterested in people who do, being apt to regard them as abnormal, self-sufficient, or recluses from choice. There may be a few of whom this is true, but the great number really suffer.

Many today – single professional women or comfortable social women (and men, too) – some of them, perhaps the last of a family, either feel driven to hold on to a long-occupied property, in a kind of loyalty, or choose to remain in a setting they know. Thanks to medical aid, penicillin, sulpha drugs and other gifts of modern science, we are all living longer. Records that still exist tell us that in Wesley's day, the average expectation of male life in Britain was about twenty-eight years, and for a woman only a little longer. Today, it is over seventy years, again with women reaching often a greater age. In Britain today, it is estimated that there are at least two million people over seventy-five, half of them living alone.

And no records are kept, as far as I know, of the young working girls and men who day after day come back from the office, and slip a key into the lock of a single room, some to make the bed they hadn't time for in the morning, to scratch together a solitary meal.

'When I was in University,' says John Pellow, in an article called 'Loneliness', 'I lived in digs. Landladies were two, of over seventy. They had two cats and they (the ladies not the cats) were both angels, but could do little for the peculiar aches and pains that a young male student has. Night after night, I walked the streets when the public library – where I studied – had closed. I walked the streets because I didn't want to go away from where there were *people*. When I could afford it, which wasn't often, I went to the pictures. Always it was to see a popular film where there were bound to be a lot of *people*. For an hour or two I would sit in the middle of a lot of *people*, and would be at ease.'

In rural areas everybody knows everybody, but in cities or large towns, we scarcely know the name of the next-door owner of the latch-key, or the family in the apartment above. Many well-meaning people, of course, are convinced that the lonely can do much more to help themselves – and in any case, they feel there isn't much time to spare for others, in this busy life.

Dietrich Bonhoeffer, who did so much for others, even to the point of giving up his life, witnessing to the reality of

the Christian Faith which prompted and enabled him, said:
'One is less lonely when one is alone.' But *he lived deeply
aware of the Living Presence of his Master, the Risen Christ*!
His words to Bonhoeffer – and to you and me – are: 'Be
assured, I am with you always' (Matthew 28:20, N.E.B.).
One needs this assurance: He is not absent because He has
ascended above the physical limitations of this earthly life
– rather is He the Everlastingly Present! *Seen* during His
stay here, He is now *unseen*, but everywhere available in
the realm of His lasting Spirit! He prepared the sensibilities
of His disciples and close friends for this whilst He was still
with them, after His resurrection. With those wonderful
words now recorded in Matthew 28:20, the assurance of
His lasting Presence, the gospel says: 'He was lifted up into
heaven. And they worshipped Him, and returned to
Jerusalem with great joy!' Rather than feel they had lost
Him, they rejoiced that from that time on they would have
His Presence in a new way. (They were not like many of
us, returning, tears streaming from our eyes, at taking
leave of a close friend at the graveyard. No! 'They returned
. . . *with great joy*', knowing that fuller, more vital
fellowship with Him would be theirs from that time on.)

And now, those of us who own ourselves His twentieth-
century disciples, lay hold of that great assurance of His:
'*Be assured, I am with you always!*'

Against any assault of loneliness, our confidence is:

> He is not far away
> Why do we sometimes seem to be alone,
> And miss the hands outstretched to meet our own?
>   He is the same today,
>   As when of old He dwelt
> In human form with His disciples – when
> He knew the needs of all His fellowmen,
>   And all their sorrows felt.

Continually Aware

Only our faith is dim,
So that our eyes are holden, and we go
All day, and until dusk before we know
That we have walked with Him.

Anon.

A Matchless Gift

In the early hours of the morning, when I left the plane at Beirut, I had some doubt about my visit. War conditions had developed since my plans were made. A message was handed to me from my missionary friend, saying that she couldn't now meet me, owing to the curfew, so would I make my own way into the city centre, where she would come when the curfew was lifted. After one or two false tries, I succeeded in securing the services of an Arab taxi boy. It was a ride I shall never forget. All along the way, uniformed men with tommy-guns lay on the flat roofs of the city buildings we passed.

When we eventually got to the Air-Centre, it was yet too early for my friend to be there. At that hour, the cleaner was sweeping the floor and emptying the ashtrays of the previous day. My documents were checked once again, and I found a chair, and settled to wait.

At last, six o'clock came, and soon after it, my friend, in the Missionary College car. We were understandably glad to see each other. Half an hour later, over breakfast, she brought forth a page of notepaper and asked me how long I could stay, and at what day and hour I would have to rejoin the plane. She wanted me to make the most of my brief stay, at the same time apologizing for the 'unsettled times'.

Suggesting several things that we might do together, she pleased me very much – and enriched me – by saying that she had procured official permission for us to make our way by car to Byblos, twenty miles north. And I shall never forget that drive by shimmering coastlines, villages, terraced vineyards, all backed by great thirsty mountains. Military patrols stopped us once or twice, but after a few minutes, allowed us to go on.

So we came to the tiny town, *the oldest continually inhabited town in the world*! And soon we were mingling with its people: first, an old man with a *fez*, then two peasant women, and a boy driving goats. Immensely thick-walled buildings told their story, as did the outline of others, reconstructed by archaeologists through the centuries. The first inhabitants of the tiny town, it seemed, had been fisher-folk, housed in a collection of rude stone huts. The natural harbour's shimmering waters had supported Phoenician sailing ships of a simple build, their likeness to be seen now only on rough, handmade museum coins. Other vessels, with the passing of the centuries, had carried from this same harbour, cargoes of cedar logs. The building needs, since Solomon built his Temple, have almost denuded the nearby Lebanon hills.

Within such a brief visit, one must imagine history unfolding, as one authority puts it, 'beginning with neolithic man seven thousand years ago, through the Bronze Age, when Byblos was at the height of its prosperity (Tyre and Sidon were, as yet, no more than simple fishing villages) until, having viewed the ruins and remains of three further millennia, one arrived breathless at the present day. A town, indeed, where Crusader and even Roman buildings can reasonably be considered "modern".'

A broken egg-shaped urn, with bones of the inhabitant of long ago, lay there exposed, preserved in the dry atmosphere, so it seemed not unfitting, macabre, or disrespectful, to photograph him as he lay comfortably at my feet on the hard surface, a stony, ill-formed way that had borne the feet of others through the passing centuries. He will, I hope, if nobody disturbs him, long be lying there.

And I reverently record my hope.

But it was none of these things which moved me to long overdue gratitude to Byblos, and made that day's ride with my friend a rich experience. The simple fact is that she is a Christian also.

Away back in the early years, BC, it seems that an Egyptian envoy visited the Phoenician town of Byblos. He was well received, and impressed by what he saw. Among the articles of trade was papyrus, derived from a simple treatment of the pith of a certain water-rush. Gathered and cut into strips, and carefully placed flat in a horizontal position, it was then covered with a second lot, vertically, after water and glue had been used. Subjected then to heavy pressure, the result in time was a writing material a little like faded brown paper, when dried and rubbed down with pumice stone.

To Byblos, I owe the name of the most precious book I have – the Bible. Papyrus – on which the Bible was first presented to the world – received its early Greek name (*byblos*, *byblinos*) from the fact that it was exported to the Aegean through Byblos. Hence the word 'Bible', derived from Byblos as 'the papyrus book'. This gift from the little town in which I spent that memorable day – whilst nearby modern hate and warlike death descended – I'll never forget.

Lots of tawdry matter pours out from the book presses, but nothing that sells as well, the world round, as this book deriving its name from little Byblos.

The reading of many today, of course, is ephemeral, serving little more purpose than to pass the time. Thinking over these things, one writer says: 'The vast reading public is made up chiefly of those who cry, "Comfort me", "Amuse me", "Touch me", "Make me shudder", "Make me laugh!"' There are times in all our lives when any one of these requests is fitting – but not all the time! And anyone who misses out altogether from his reading a place for that Greatest Book of all, is wasteful. I think of this every time I hear the sweet, thin voices of the children in church, in:

> God has given us a Book full of stories,
>   Which was made for His people of old,
> It begins with the tale of a garden,
>   And ends with the city of gold.
>
> But the best is the story of Jesus,
>   Of the Babe, with the ox in the stall,
> Of the song that was sung by the angels,
>   The most beautiful story of all.

But it is not only a book for children – far from it. At the Coronation of our Royalty I have heard the Bible referred to as 'the most valuable thing this world affords'. Is that a meaningless boast? I hope not, although I fear that for many in our midst it is. This arises, perhaps, out of the much that is made of our *duty* to read the Bible, so that many read it as 'a task enjoined', rather than as 'a delight enjoyed'. Countless eyebrows went up, I observed, when Anthony Deane wrote a book with the title *How to Enjoy the Bible*. Was it a misprint? No, it wasn't!

Another hindrance to the would-be reader of the Bible, is the tendency to begin at the wrong place, by starting at the beginning as with any ordinary book. The simple stories of Genesis, even Exodus, the readers can enjoy – that is if they don't balk at the lack of scientific data in dealing with the creation of the world. But the Bible is not a single book meant to be read straight through: it's a library, in every form of literature – an old-world story, with which it begins, history, poetry, drama, song, hymns,

prayers, love stories, letters and
these, each needs its own approac.
book.

A good idea is to start with the New Tes.
failed to get any further than, say, Leviticus,
as a result of starting the Bible immediately ins.
cover. And start, not with Matthew, but with   .k's
gospel, the oldest in point of time, and full of eagerness;
so you will come upon those lively words 'straightway', and
'immediately', and be introduced to a 'young man
running'. And it's full of action: fewer words of Jesus, more
of His doings! For that reason, it's the best book to start
a young person on, or a person coming to Bible reading for
the first time, or after a break.

Alternately – after some knowledge of Jesus – it is good
to start with an unbroken reading of Acts. It's a thrilling
story of the remarkable and courageous things that
happened to those who followed Him!

Get a Bible with a coloured cover, and good print, of
course. For sheer literary beauty the Authorized Version
stands unchallenged, as 'the best words of the best period
of English, in the best order'. Read it, and see! But if you
are inclined to stumble over words in our language that
have changed their meaning as they've come up through
the centuries, try one of the modern versions. There are
any number of them, that come to us as a gift from God,
through scholarly, true, devoted men. After the
Authorized Version that I was brought up on, my favourite
of them all is the Revised Standard Version.

The Good Old Days

After a long drive, I came thankfully to St Christopher's, Harpenden. My friend hadn't dropped the blinds, though she had lighted the reading lamp, and it made a pretty sight as I walked up the drive. A moment later, in answer to my knock, I was welcomed in.

'What's happened to your old grandfather-clock?' was almost my first word. 'He isn't going.'

'Oh,' replied my friend, 'one of his weights fell off. I fixed it. But', she added with a chuckle, 'I must have done something a bit wrong; he immediately began to go backwards. Do you know anything about clocks?'

'Not much,' I had to confess, 'but I'm pretty sure they shouldn't go backwards.'

Some, of course, would like them to: 'Backward, turn backward, O Time in your flight, Make me a child again, just for tonight.' Even some Christians talk that way, but it's no use harking back to 'the Good Old Days'. 'The happy day that fix'd my choice' is gone; this is another day!

'Marvellous things did He in the sight of the fathers, and in the land of Egypt.' But He is God still, in this age of the atom, of growing literacy, of Church unity. These are great days! Why turn the clock back? What's the point?

Our Christian Faith is an on-going experience – it is not belief in spite of evidence, but 'Life in scorn of consequence'.

> 'Give us this day our daily bread' we pray,
> And give us likewise, Lord, our daily thought,
> That our poor souls may strengthen as they ought,
> And starve not on the husks of yesterday.

That is a good prayer; we can't go back to what we once believed, *we must go onward* in our thought, matching this age in which we live. It was said of the quaint old schoolmaster, Domine Bobiensis, by Marryat: 'He breathed in the present age, but lived most of his time in antiquity.' And to this hour, we are acquainted with some of his kith and kin, even within the church pew, which they fill pretty faithfully the years through. But their religion belongs back in the Old Testament days; there they feel at home, with the Ten Commandments – they like to swing back there. But our Lord and Master has given us a further word: 'Thou shalt love the Lord thy God with all thy heart, and with all thy soul, and with all thy mind. This is the first and great commandment. And the second is like unto it. *Thou shalt love thy neighbour as thyself. On these two commandments hang all the Law and the Prophets*' (Matthew 22:37–40, A.V.).

In ever so many ways, it's good to have a knowledge of the past – what we often call 'the Good Old Days' – though there is no living reason why we should want to go backwards to Old Testament times, or into our grandparents' days. What was so good about them? There was peace in the countryside, of course, and unpolluted air; one could breathe deeply without hurt, and look at the stars by night, with no hindrance from headlights of dashing motors, or neon lights along the buildings of business areas. It was very pleasant then to travel as slowly as one wished, and take notice of the country sights – though a good deal of the road one travelled was liable to be rutted.

And there was health to be considered. Dr Roger Pilkington, of our day, says in his *Heavens Alive*, 'Occasionally people will murmur about the good old days, but for whom were these old days so good? For those', he answers, 'lucky enough not to die in childbirth or of gangrene, or to see their families expire one by one of dysentery, typhus, or some other epidemic. The good old days before science was beginning to have an effect upon life were, to my mind, very bad old days indeed; and if anyone should think it was all a matter of *gay galliards and shepherd's hey*, let him look up and see how many children our poor Queen Anne bore, none of whom survived adolescence.

'Compare our life today with what it was only a century ago, and it is at once obvious what we owe to the application of scientific knowledge. Hygiene, sewage disposal and public health research have doubled the average length of life (in the West) within a century. Not only our life, but every member of our body is extended in efficiency by gadgets of astonishing ingenuity, worked out by science. We can lift huge weights with gigantic cranes. With the microscope the resolving power of our eyes is so revolutionized that we can see bacteria, even viruses. The telescope enables us to study the actual appearance of parts of the universe as they were some eight million years ago. With television we can see instantaneously from one place to another a hundred miles away, or – with Telstar – across the Atlantic Ocean. Plastics, synthetic fibres, drugs, brain surgery, refrigerators, automobiles, teleprinters, jet aircraft – these and a thousand other things have changed our way of life.'

'A young sister of my mother', John Oxenham confessed, looking back only a little way in our day, 'lived with us all her life. She was deemed almost too advanced . . . because of a book she bought and read in the privacy of her room. It was *Jane Eyre*. It was her great standby for years. I imagine now that whenever the monotony of our small household got too much for her, she would indulge in a wild orgy of *Jane Eyre*.'

The author of *Jane Eyre* herself knew much monotony in the life she shared in the Brontë parsonage. And when she learned that it was the lot of many other single women, she wrote of their plight. 'And when I speak thus', said she, knowing well that she would be counted too daring, 'I have no impression that I displease God by my words; that I am neither impious or impatient, irreligious or sacrilegious. Look at the numerous families of girls . . . The brothers of these girls are every one in business or in professions; they have something to do; their sisters have no earthly employment but household work and sewing; no earthly pleasure but an unprofitable visiting; and no hope, in all their life, to come of anything better.'

Who of us – single by choice, having come to the crossroads several times – would go back to those womanly limitations, and from the vantage of our present-day professional life, speak of those earlier times as 'the Good Old Days'?

Though many of our moral and spiritual values have slipped – and this is to be regretted – our horizons, these days, are much wider than they used to be.

> Thank God our time is *now*, when wrong
> Rises to face us everywhere . . .
> Affairs are now soul-size!

Forgive Us . . . As We Forgive!

Many of us think forgiveness is a fine idea – until there is someone to forgive, and then it's a different matter.

'Jesus', says Bishop Gerald Kennedy, as straightforwardly as I've heard him say many other things, 'brings us a vision of God's love for the sinner. He shows us also the terrible cost of forgiveness. Someone may say that God could simply forgive men and let it go at that. Then we must answer that until men have some sense of what forgiveness means, forgiveness cannot save them.

'A man', he adds, 'may have been bad in his own life; he may hold no high standards of how to act. Then he may forgive another man simply because the man's sin is no worse than what he himself has been doing all along. The man who is forgiven in this way will think the forgiveness has little value . . . But here is another person who has lived a pure life and hates an evil act with all his heart. Let this man forgive the sinner, and the guilty one falls to his knees in an agony of repentance. It is then a terrible thing to be forgiven. But it is a saving thing' (*I Believe*, Abingdon Press, pp. 22f).

Forgiveness is costly! Following that part of the Lord's Prayer where we cry for our daily bread, is this cry for forgiveness. No one, anywhere in our present-day needy world, questions our need of bread, though in many parts where this prayer rises, bread is desperately hard to find. (And so, you might well interject, is forgiveness.) *Our Father God's forgiveness, and our human forgiveness*, are eternally tied together! The words of this prayer given to us, and more widely known than any other the world round, are: 'Father forgive us . . . as we forgive' (Matthew 6:12, A.V.). There is no missing the costliness of forgiveness.

It is the only petition tied to an obligation – how can we pray it glibly, casually? So much turns upon it: our Lord and Master, who first set it upon man's lips, made the family obligation of forgiveness unmistakable – and we are all members of God's family on earth! God's heavenly forgiveness, and our earthly forgiveness, are now forever joined – and no man can put them asunder. Hearts that in daily affairs harbour fault-finding, hot hate, and bitter spite, are in no fit state to receive the Father's forgiveness.

But how do we forgive? 'We belong to an imperfect world', Evelyn Underhill tenderly but firmly reminds us, in her widely accepted book, *Abba*, meaning '*Father*'. 'That downward pull, that declension from the light, which theology calls "original sin", is felt at every level of our being. With the deepening of our experience we become more and more conscious of this . . .' And since this is a daily business it is something that we have to learn in a practical way. In Coventry, certain members of the one-time enemy air force have been welcomed back to the city in peacetime, on the principle of this great dual petition: 'FATHER FORGIVE!' It is hard to do, in greater or lesser degree, wherever harm between men and women has been done, and cruel hurt suffered.

But in this earth, there are no two words more relevant, though we know that there are some things that forgiveness cannot undo. It cannot call back the past, as though it had never been spoiled – the opportunity missed, the cruel word spoken, the merciless deed done, now are part of history, and the pattern of personal living. Nor can forgiveness remove a total disposition to sin. Once forgiven, it may flare again, a display of fierce temper, a passion for strong drink, for damaging drugs, for

debauchery and destruction. In the closest personal sense
– as between father and child, husband and wife, friend and
friend – it does not cease to be reality. Forgiveness cannot
ignore the consequences of a misused body, a strained
nervous system, a scattered fortune. It requires a new
evaluation of things based on love, not hate, spite, getting
even. And that is as true of the Heavenly Father's
relationship with any one of us!

But it is a wonderful thing when, in this involved world
of relationships, we find happenings that tell us how
beautifully, healingly real is forgiveness.

Modern-day examples keep coming to the fore, and they
strengthen us. For years I have had meetings, from time to
time, with the Reverend Dr David Coles, now Dean of
Waipu, living near the Cathedral in Napier, where that
New Zealand city rises anew, after a great disaster. I knew
Dr Coles first as a young priest in a small suburban church
where I was invited to speak. He gathered us first that
morning for the Eucharist. It was a united gathering, for
he was even then a good sharer. Later, he came to the
church where I regularly worship, to lecture at an
ecumenical gathering. Later still, I worshipped at another
such gathering in the big church of St Peter's, where he
then ministered. And this morning I broke into my typing
of this chapter on forgiveness, to listen to his voice coming
into our lounge, on the mid-morning radio session 'Faith
for Today'. He told a wonderful modern-day story, and I
wrote to him, asking if I could use it, and here it is.

He began: 'We've just had a couple of really interesting
people staying at our house. John and Audrey Coleman
were hostages in Iran. You remember when all the
American Embassy staff were held hostage a couple of
years ago. Well, a handful of British people were also taken
at that time, including Dr Coleman and his wife. They were
held prisoner for two hundred days before they were

released in February last year. And they were only released after the intervention of the Archbishop of Canterbury.

'The Colemans gave nearly twenty years of their lives to the people of Iran, as medical missionaries, running clinics and a hospital. What really impressed me was the way they bear no malice towards those who held them prisoner. *They've been able to forgive their captors. They've not only forgiven them, but they still have a deep love for those people.*

'That's what the Christian Faith teaches. Jesus said: "If one of the occupation troops forces you to carry his pack one kilometre, carry it two kilometres" . . . "Love your enemies and pray for those who persecute you, so that you may become sons of your Father in heaven." I guess', finished Dr Coles, 'that's why Jesus taught us in the Lord's Prayer, to pray that God will forgive our sins, as we forgive those who sin against us.'

Private and Purposeful

Do you keep a diary? Or is this a question I shouldn't ask? I know it's a very private matter. I kept one myself, for many years, and very purposefully, beginning in my childhood and continuing right up into my early twenties.

I just don't remember the year but I got my first from Father Christmas, and it had a bright red cover. A very tiny diary it was, but I was very excited! There weren't always many heroic things to enter, and almost always a lack of important names – we lived in a quiet country part – but there were games, and mushrooming, and picnics, and blackberry-picking, and prizes at school – all that sort of thing.

It didn't take me long to learn the basic truth: there was room in diary-keeping for big, brave happenings and sayings, and for little, commonplace things. It was helping me to learn what life was like, day by day. The very name 'diary', my dictionary said, came from the Latin *diarium*, *dies*, a day.

Another – a little bright green one – came the next Christmas, the same size, with the same opportunities. Then, there came a blue-covered one. I liked, each Christmas morning, when I wakened early to attend to my stocking, to find there another little diary from Father Christmas. He never failed me – even more, he believed in me, in my perseverance. He must have known how eager I was each year to start again, and how hard it was to keep on to the thirty-first of December. I liked that. And I liked even more the fact that the Old Gentleman never once came around about September to see what I was doing with his gift – if, indeed, I was doing anything! 'No one', I found a famous English writer, Charles Lamb, quoted in a book at school as saying, 'ever regarded the First of January with indifference!' True! Especially, it seemed, a diary-keeper: there were so many things to get on to the small page at the beginning, with guests staying, and gifts, and special things to eat! But in the new books that awaited us in the library, when we went back to school, I happened on a kindred spirit who found it hard to keep going, after the end of January. (I should say that years on, when I found myself confined to bed for many, many months with 'a germ on my heart', I had to give up diary-keeping; though I've always kept an interest in other diary-keepers.) Among others, I happened on a book: *The Season of the Year*, published by Collins, later to be my own publisher. There, the diarist, John Moore – looking back to his earliest efforts – confessed: 'It is depressing to discover how little I have changed.' He had noticed a little entry: 'Had a cold!' That seemed as short as could be, after a gap – and rather bleak. Soon, there was nothing more engaging than a poorly-spelled entry about the family canaries: 'There feet are pinkish white, and their beaks are whitish pink. They sing with great buity, and hope about on there perch.'

And years on, I find Ethel Mannin – writer of many books, which of itself requires a great deal of perseverance – confessing in her *Connemara Journal* (Westhouse, London, p. 107): 'The keeping of a day-to-day diary can be exceedingly boring; far from being an escape, a refuge, it becomes a most tedious labour; one gets behind with the wretched thing, and then cannot remember what one did the day before yesterday, and has a sense of having mislaid a day, regardless of the fact that one has had it and lived it . . . How the great diarists like Evelyn and Pepys and Fanny Burney kept up their diaries for years, I cannot imagine, except from force of habit – for it does, in time, become that, a habit.' 'Nothing peculiar happened today', becomes an entry by many, not only M. Vivian Hughes in her book *A London Diary*.

Samuel Pepys, the most famous of our diarists, found continuance of his task a challenge, and kept it up faithfully, using a contrived shorthand to serve 'privacy', if not the 'purposeful' nature of his undertaking, for nine busy years! This compares interestingly with the effort of the great John Evelyn, who kept his diary entries going for sixty-four years!

But, of course, as in life – length isn't all! There is something remarkably colourful about Pepys's entries. 'Vitality', one person writes, introducing him to us, 'the first and the only unfakeable element of literature, he has.' So perhaps length in a diary, or in life, doesn't matter most – it is *quality* that does that!

For nearly a hundred years, six of Pepys's small books, containing some three thousand pages, lay undisturbed in a library at Magdalene College, Cambridge. Then, Lord Grenville, showing a lively interest in them, handed them over to an undergraduate, one John Smith. All quite ordinary sounding – but Smith tackled the seemingly impossible task of deciphering the record of Pepys's interests, observations, and doings public and personal, from January 1659 to 31 May 1669. And the surprising outcome was published a couple of years later – and was received as a classic.

Among others of fame who have joined Evelyn and Pepys, and Sir William Dugdale, an enterprising Warwickshire gentleman devoted to diary-keeping, are a cluster of names known to us: Fanny Burney, bright and nimble, breaking new ground; and Nancy Woodforde, of a famous, widely known family. It has been claimed by experts on the matter that 'it is probable that between 1800 and 1820, there can hardly have been a day on which one

Woodforde or another did not note down what he ate for dinner, or what the weather was like, or that the harvest was carried, or that the tailor over-charged him for mending a waistcoat.' There must have been more time in those days – and more energy!

C. S. Lewis, in our century – much loved for his Christian spirit, honoured for his many lectures, his broadcasts, and many books – doubtless knew the achievements of all these famous diarists I've named. But he finds space in his autobiography, *Surprised by Joy*, for his own opinion. In that book, on the shelves of most of us, he confesses: 'A diary is nothing like so useful as I had hoped. You put down each day what you think important; *but of course you cannot each day see what will prove to have been important in the long run.*'

True! It is this, of course, that Christopher Morley pauses to underline for us, in one of his neat little verses:

> Never write up your diary
>   On the day itself;
> It takes longer than that
>   To know what happened.

But chances are, alas, that if one doesn't do it on the day on which something of interest happens, it will be skipped altogether. There is, nevertheless, a lot of truth in that little verse. *One needs to learn in life to keep things in perspective.* One thinks of one's hero, Captain Scott of the Antarctic, modern keeper of some of the most moving diaries we have. 'Early in June,' he tells us – though the importance of it never dawned on him at the time – 'I was spending my short leave in London, and chanced one day to walk down the Buckingham Palace Road. I espied Sir Clement Markham on the opposite pavement, and naturally crossed, and as naturally turned and accompanied him to his home. That afternoon, I learned for the first time that there was such a thing as a prospective Antarctic expedition; *two days later*, I wrote applying to command it.'

'The last diary of Captain Scott is good to read,' wrote Kate O'Brien, editor of *English Diaries and Journals*, 'as a reminder of the power of courage, and the dignity of men. Everyone knows the magnificent story of the last journey to the South Pole, and whoever knows the story knows the diary . . . found on the Barrier . . . The entries of the last two months are immortal.'

It is easy to bypass perspective, and that would be a shame – it is so important in this life.

It is a long time since I first learned that oblong is my favourite shape for a gift. But does Father Christmas still distribute diaries in pretty colours at Christmas? I don't know, but I hope so – there's so much to be learned that way, for life!

We Live!

I cannot now remember the day, the hour, when first I came upon a book by the widely loved novelist Dorothy Canfield. All I know is that from that moment a new expectation and a new realization were implanted in my spirit.

Some time ago, an outsider, visiting the Vermont countryside, stopped at Arlington to buy something he needed. Looking about him, before he took off again, he noticed a woman walking along near him. And with some superiority, he questioned her: 'What on earth do you do in a sleepy little town like this?' The woman was Dorothy Canfield. She answered him firmly and gladly: 'We live!'

The reality of life – the quality of it – has very little to do with geography!

Jesus, our Lord, grew up in a little place called Nazareth, on the Palestinian hillside. I have been there, have walked its modest streets, and sought out, for His sake, a carpenter's workshop, such as was His daily setting, amid the piled timbers, pieces of finished work, and sweet wood-shavings. There, for years after Bethlehem, His birth-place, and life as a refugee in Egypt, that was His setting.

Nazareth was an insignificant little place, many would have said; not even mentioned in the Old Testament Scriptures. 'Could any good come out of Nazareth?' someone asked later, when he heard that Jesus, calling men, had come from there (John 1:46). The answer that he received was the only satisfactory answer: 'Come and see!' He did – and never forgot it.

That was the kind of answer Dorothy Canfield gave.

'What do we do? We live!' It was not just a matter of words; she well knew that the quality of that life would speak for itself.

Here and now, wherever we are living, our life may do the same, if we can truly say, in the richest possible sense, 'We live!' Geography never need hold one back, country, town, swathed with every possible encouragement, every satisfaction, or at the mercy of spite, and desperate opposition. No less a young Christian of our day than Dietrich Bonhoeffer, who fell into the hands of the Nazis, had something unforgettable to say about this business called living. He said: 'I would like to speak of God, *not on the borders of life, but at its centre*; not in weakness, but in strength; not in man's suffering and death, but in his life and prosperity.' He wants life, above all, to be a witness of steady values, even as the life of his young Lord was, in that little town of Nazareth.

I haven't any doubt that there were times when it bored Him, when 'He went to worship, as His custom was', and the rabbi drawled on wearily, for Jesus was young, so much alive, so much devoted to lasting values. He might have been set to learn His trade, and serve in the most-loved city of all – Jerusalem – in one of its arched lanes, where to this day are workbenches with diminished light filtering through. But no! That wouldn't have been as meaningful. From the beginning, God the Father had intended to set Him down in an ordinary little place, Nazareth, and He grew up there, his parents well-known and the neighbours sharing the comings and goings of every day.

When He put up the shutters of His little workshop for the last time, and went out to preach and to heal, men and women asked: 'Is not this the carpenter's son? Is not His mother called Mary?' (Matthew 13:55–56, A.V.). 'And His brothers, James, and Joses, and Simon, and Judas?

And His sisters, are they not all with us?' Even the devils knew that He lived in Nazareth (Mark 1:21–24, A.V.). Once He and His company of friends went into Capernaum, 'And straightway, on the Sabbath day, He entered into the synagogue and taught. And they were astonished at His doctrine: for He taught them as one that had authority, and not as the scribes. And there was in the synagogue a man with an unclean spirit: and he cried out, saying: "Let us alone: what have we to do with thee, thou Jesus of Nazareth?"'

If one could but spare one word to sum up Jesus's ministry, that word would be '*Life*'! He was so young, so full of vitality, so eager, so compassionate. He came at last to Death, His ministry crowned, and beyond Death to Fuller Life, without a single silver strand on His head that He carried so splendidly!

Dr Charles Raven was only one to say of Him, in our day: 'He would have drawn a boy like me to His feet. He is so plainly the hero that I wanted, the hero who was not merely strong, but sensitive and sympathetic, brave and yet tragic, lonely and wholly lovable . . . If only my teachers had not put a halo on His head, and talked affectedly, or not at all, about Him!'

Exactly!

Christ's captivating call walked up and down in the minds of many a one with whom He had dealings: '*I came*', *said He*, '*that they may have life, and that they may have it abundantly*' (John 10:10, A.V.). Against the laboured dullness and wordiness of the piety of His day, this was glorious. Literal observances of the Law were widespread; but here was something vastly bigger, and more vital.

By 'life' he meant a new existence, become possible to ordinary people, not only in the place of worship, but in the setting of daily work. Men and women have always tried to find words in which to sum it up, and to this day, we keep on doing that. Dr Adolf Harnack says it better than any other, so far as I have discovered: 'The Christian religion', he says, '*is something simple and sublime. It means one thing, and one thing only – eternal Life in the midst of Time, by the strength, and under the eyes of God!*'

I could never have dreamed that 'another of the greats of our day' – Lord Reith of the BBC – would have had to confess less. But there is now no forgetting John Freeman's interview with him, 'Face to Face'. Questioned, 'Do you have any regrets?', Lord Reith lifted up that great granite head of his, to answer, 'Yes; for discovering too late that *life is for living!*'

Free Choice

Today, I've had a birthday, or at least, half a birthday, being a twin. I have only once ever had a whole one to myself, and that was when I chanced to be in London, in Tilbury, joining ship for home. Being on the other side of the world, with each day coming earlier, my twin sister had already had her birthday and gone to bed. Then, in London, I began to celebrate. I enjoyed the novelty of it, although, of course, I had no choice.

As small schoolgirls, we contended also that having our 'birth-date' near Christmas, as far as gifts were concerned we were to suffer from it all our lives. For Christmas, we might get lovely storybooks, balls, puzzles, and each an orange in her stocking, with a shiny sixpence tucked into the toe. But a birthday was another thing altogether. If we were lucky, we might each get a pair of sandals; new pencils; new class-books – which we always said, under our breaths, we would have got anyhow.

Early in January in our area was harvest time, fruit-picking and jam-making time, and our parents hadn't much time to give to celebratory surprises. Gifts were a matter of 'Hobson's Choice', not really a choice at all, only an acceptance of whatever came, in the best spirit we knew.

Old Thomas Hobson, it seemed, had lived in Cambridge, England. Life was good enough to him, and he was able, from time to time, to give coins to the poor about him; a piece of building land to the city's University; and a large Bible to the church of St Benedict. He even lent money to the King, when His Majesty needed aid. And the populace honoured citizen Thomas Hobson. In time, there was a street blessed with his name; and a Conduit, standing at the centre of the marketplace. No one could overlook such good deeds.

Thomas Hobson's father had been a carrier; and when he died, his eight fine horses, the cart, and the carrier's business between Cambridge and London, fell to his son. The fifty-six miles journey each way seemed, in those days, a long way. Roads were roughly surfaced, and sometimes dangerous, not only because of holes and ruts, but because of lurking highwaymen. Hobson carried to and fro not only parcels and letters, but as many passengers as he could manage. Generally, it was a rather uncomfortable journey. Some who wished to cover the distance, elected to ride horseback, and to go when time suited them.

Hobson – wide awake – bought more horses, and set about hiring them out. He earned notice by being the first man in England to think of doing such a thing, and the idea soon took on. (Whether his own boys and girls, of whom there were eight, ever enjoyed a free ride, there is no record.) But many horse lovers in Cambridge hired from him, and many of his riders were students from the University. In a life full of lectures and books, it was exciting to ride, and soon the good stablemaster had to provide more horses. It was at this point, that he became famous for what came to be known as 'Hobson's Choice'.

Some of his horses were quiet and gentle, others frisky and dangerous. He noticed that when certain young men from the University came to hire them, they liked to choose the best ones, or at least, those they had ridden before. In that way, some horses got ridden too much, and some hardly enough to keep them in good fettle. So their wise old master made a rule: always when a would-be rider came to hire, the next horse to go out was the next one in the stable. No one was allowed to choose his 'fancy mount' – it was 'Hobson's Choice', or nothing. And horse lovers in and around Cambridge never forgot it. It wasn't really a choice at all – *they just had to accept what was given them*.

In some senses, life treats us like that – we none of us choose our parents, our birthdays, our names, even whether we shall have white skins. We cannot even select our own sex.

In a great area of our life here, nevertheless, *God has given us His great gift of Choice*. And this lifts us above creatures of the animal kingdom, so widely and wonderfully spread about this earth of His. There is no unbending compulsion in our relationship with Him, no 'Hobson's Choice' about it. Lord Gorell has said it once and for all: 'God is no Master of puppets, nor need we dance to His tune.' He has endowed us each with the right to make our own choice – even to refuse His claims upon our lives, though He is our Creator, and through Christ, our Redeemer. Our Christianity turns on a glorious Choice: those of us who find ourselves entering into it, in this earthly life, find it is an adventure of Love – and one cannot compel Love.

One by one, men and women up through the long centuries to this very hour, have recorded this for us, as life's most glorious Choice. Some of them have not been content simply to raise their voices, but they have written books. Two who have done both, are C. S. Lewis and David Sheppard – a university lecturer, and a much loved English cricketer, now a bishop. Said Lewis in an unforgettable section of one of his books: 'I was offered what now appears *a moment of wholly free choice* . . . I could open the door, or keep it shut . . . . no threat or promise was attached to either, though I knew that to open the door meant the incalculable.'

In his turn, David Sheppard spoke of *his hour of choice*: 'I walked back to my rooms in Trinity Hall late at night. I knew that it was more important than anything else in the world that I should become right with God. I knelt . . . and asked Christ to come into my life, to forgive me, and to be my Friend and Master.' And this world is full of others of us who have each a like story to tell.

The glory of it is that He with Whom we have to do is not 'a divine puppeteer', controlling us, in every choice, at His own will. We none of us dance at the end of a string.

Ernest Jeffs, not waiting to write a book, set it out compellingly in a Christian newspaper that came regularly through my letterbox at a critical time. 'I mean', said he, 'that we deliberately *choose Christ* to be our Master, irrespective of the question of His authority – of any authority, that is, apart from what we actually see Him to be. We perceive that there are more views than one as to His divinity, as to the meaning of His death, as to the fact of His resurrection, as to the details and interpretation of his teaching. Never mind. Seeing Him, as we do see Him, against the background of history, against the background of thought, against the background of the present-day world, and of our own lives and our own natures, we quite deliberately – quite arbitrarily, if you will – decide to become His followers: to stand or fall with Him, to live or die with Him: to find in the end that what He said of God was true, or to find that it was false or mistaken: to take all the risks of believing in Him enough to follow Him *without any authority except His Person, and our own free choice*.'

Nothing more need be said – but what a glorious truth it is!

Just Where We Are!

I was guest at a gathering of folk, lately – retired ministers and their wives, retired deaconesses, missionaries. There was lively talk as I walked in, and out of the company towards me came one smiling face. Greeting me, her latest news was of a stay in hospital, and a word of thanksgiving that she was now back home. 'I want to tell you', she began, 'that I took with me my loved copy of *Prayers in After Life*. And it was such a help, with its large type.'

I interrupted her, at this point, with a twinkle in my eye: 'Wouldn't it be *Prayers in Later Life*?' And we both smiled at the mistitling of my book. I could never write a book about prayers in the After Life – once in the immediate presence of our Lord and Saviour, would there be need for prayers, unless for Praise and Adoration? But there was certainly need for prayers here, we both knew that. And there was something that we could share in such a book.

It was one thing to talk 'about God', and another thing to talk 'to God'. For that is what prayer means to us here on earth, and it is a wonderful experience. We never know all of it, though it can begin simply. I love the way Dr H. H. Farmer speaks of it: 'You are going to give ten minutes to prayer in your room. It is very quiet and very familiar and very commonplace there. There is the furniture, the bed, the gas bracket, a grey sky outside, perhaps even a bluebottle buzzing on the windowpane. Take five minutes to read one of the stories of Jesus, or a brief passage from a book about Jesus. Just read it, and visualize Jesus, and reverence Him. That is all. You look up. The room is just the same. Nothing has happened outwardly. You have heard no voice, felt no presence. The bluebottle is still buzzing. Have you wasted your time? Not for a moment. You have communed with God through Jesus Christ. In the deeper places of your spirit, you are better and stronger.'

Another as tellingly urges that communion of spirit be sought at the opening of each day. Thinking of God, much as Dr Farmer does, he says:

> Give Him thy first thoughts;
> So shalt thou keep
> Him company all day,
> And in Him sleep.

For many others, prayer is more often than not a crisis affair. It is like grasping something firm when suddenly they find themselves falling. I always think of this as a very low expression of prayer, although it can be very real. It is likely to be erratic, for life goes on happily enough for most of us, day after day. Nobody we love falls sick; no accident occurs; nobody in our immediate circle is frightened out of her wits; no one suddenly loses his job; and following George Herbert's claim, nobody goes to sea. In his day, of course, it was a hazardous experience. 'He who will learn to pray,' were George Herbert's words, 'let him go to sea.' Was that how he himself learned? I'm not sure – all I know is that he was a very good Christian man, and that he prayed.

In our day, one's major fear may more likely come from collision with a speeding car, or involvement in a plane smash, or train accident. This is such an age of speed. Long, slow journeys are out of favour these days – we like to visualize ourselves ripping along. I know of at least one schoolmistress who remembers one of her young scribes setting down in one of his essays: 'Speed is a fine thing, speed is.' He is not wholly to be blamed – he might have a father or an uncle in an admired business position who is 'proud to arrive in Hong Kong still smoking the packet of cigarettes he bought at Idlewild'. In George Herbert's day, of course, he would not be travelling at any greater speed than that of a horse-and-gig at most. But then, in those days, patients in scores of parishes would be dying of diphtheria.

Men and women prayed in any crisis of the kind I have hinted at, and in many an instance it was so common and widespread, that church doors were open at all hours, so that people could go in and pray. We still have a few of these national crises, and then we pack our pews.

In hate-drenched areas, as in parts of Ireland, death all too often descends suddenly through bomb reprisals; and there are as well the war-cursed lands where mass death by genocide is a grim reality. Our overall capacity to annihilate our fellows has become so ghastly efficient. For all that medical skills, and aids like X-ray, electro-cardiograms, blood banks and all manner of modern means have become available, family crisis is all too real. Nowhere is there a ward where by night and day prayer does not ascend. Though crisis prayer is not the only kind of prayer, nor is it the highest, though desperately real!

We can think of the ineffable Being of God – the Almighty and meticulous creator of mountains, galaxies, and minute wild flowers, and the tiny fingernails of an infant. Adoration and thanksgiving come uppermost in our prayers at such a time. Our quest for guidance is another form of prayer – what we call *petition*. More general still, though not more natural, is *intercession*: praying for others. One can help most by unhurriedly visualizing the needy one as we know him or her, and the situation which is known to be at the present, and so lovingly, imaginatively, trustfully bring the need to God. Think how it would be, if there were no God, all-loving, all-wise, all-willing, at such times!

But we must not overlook *confession*, whether we put it in first, middle, or last. We need bravely, honestly to acknowledge our weakness, our sins, before our all-loving Father, God. And at this time it is a pity, though easier, to use portmanteau phrases like 'Forgive me all my sins'. It takes some courage to enumerate individual offences; it makes one blush to mention mean-speaking behind another's back, for instance. And to think one has now been a Christian for fifteen years, or forty, or fifty-five!

First, and always, in prayer, one must make an important place for *acknowledgement*, and *praise*: 'Our Father, which art in Heaven, hallowed be Thy Name; Thy Kingdom come, Thy Will be done in Earth, as it is in Heaven!'

There are always times when simple ejaculatory prayer is right – even if, perhaps, less beautiful than that of the ancient Prayer Book, or even a more modern one, like the large-type one I wrote myself, with a title that my dear friend confused, *Prayers in Later Life*. I have found much help at times in the beautiful Collects of the Book of Common Prayer, as in a little cluster of modern-day prayers on my bedside shelf: prayers by Dr W. E. Orchard, or Dr Walter Rauschenbusch, and more recently, those by Dr John Baillie, or Dr William Barclay. But I like best private prayers, unprinted, although they use the best speech of one's best moments. They more easily strike a note of relevance – and that is always essential. There are times when *silent prayer* serves to refresh one's spirit. Elizabeth Leseur, a French woman, a Catholic, married to an unbeliever, though an intellectual, found this to be marvellously true. She kept a journal called *A Wife's Story*. One of the entries that tells of its refreshing purpose is: 'To forget myself for all. *To renew every day* from our Saviour my too soon exhausted store of tenderness, strength and serenity. To increase in gentleness, and make myself more welcoming to all when, as now, I long ardently for solitude and silence and rest. To try at the same time to have as many moments of recollectedness as possible so that my soul may have the nourishment it needs so much, which makes it strong and peaceable and full of spiritual life.'

Wherever we pray – or however – we do not know ahead what God's answers will be; but we do know what His attitude is!

A Great Time To Be Alive!

It was a blue-sky day, and my little car was running sweetly. The good Leicestershire miles brought me to Staunton Harold. Soon, I was being served tea in the ancient manor, said to derive its name from Saxon holders in days before the Conquest. The ageing master of Staunton Hall eagerly explained how he had just bought a replacement for Bottesford's bellrope, as his ancestors had done time and again. 'It's the tenor bellrope', said the old gentleman, as we examined together a piece of the discarded rope. 'Out of curiosity,' he then added, 'I've been looking up costs. A new one in the eighteenth century cost five shillings [25 pence], in the nineteenth, seven-and-six [37½ pence], now in the twentieth, five pounds!' And I learned not only how much the cost of keeping alert had gone up; but how Staunton came to have an obligation to pay for a bellrope for Bottesford Church. I was curious.

It seemed that an ancestor of my host received the lands of Staunton from the standard-bearer of William the Conqueror, on one condition. Seven miles distant is Belvoir Castle, and in between them, Bottesford Church. 'Whenever the reigning monarch came to the castle,' I was told, 'a flag was flown. Then Staunton of Staunton had to ride over with a golden key. But', he went on to explain, 'the mists might be down, or it might be night. Then, instead of a flag being run up, a bell had to be rung. It would be heard at Bottesford Church, and there the tenor bell would be rung – and here, finally, we got the call at Staunton! That has been the plan for hundreds of years!'

I was fascinated. But more so with the inscription over

the doorway of Staunton Church itself – claimed, by those who love it, to be one of the most unspoiled in all Leicestershire.

It was built by Sir Robert Shirley, during hard times, when few buildings were going up. Still, the inscription over its doorway tells its story:

> In the year 1653
> when all things sacred were throughout the nation
> either demolished or profaned,
> Sir Robert Shirley, Baronet,
> founded this church,
> whose singular praise it is
> to have done *the best things in the worst times*
> and hoped them in the most calamitous . . .

Those seven simple words carry a God-like quality to confront one when in an excuse-making mood. We all, from time to time, know that mood: when it comes to put off a planned undertaking or delay a good deed till things are better. But Sir Robert Shirley didn't do that. I speak of his action as 'a God-like action'. And to support my praise, I turn to my Bible. When God's great Gift to this world of ours was due to be given us, '*God did the best things in the worst times*'. Soon after His birth, Herod sought out the human-divine Babe with bloody ferocity, sending specially ordered soldiers to the task.

On a day this world will never forget, three Wise Men, at the end of a special God-sent journey, sought Herod's help in finding the place where the infant Prince should be born. But Herod had no adequate answer for them, only a request that when they had found Him, they should return, so that Herod could worship Him too, although he had no such intention. 'And being warned in a dream not to return to Herod, they departed to their own country by another way' (Matthew 2:12, R.S.V.). 'Then Herod, when he saw that he had been tricked by the Wise Men, was in a furious rage, and he sent and killed all the male children in Bethlehem and in all the region who were two years old or under' (Matthew 2:16, R.S.V.).

But despite man's spite and rage adding up to 'the worst of times', God's good Gift made it one of this world's 'best things'.

The revelation of the Cross is a like story, showing 'the best things' in 'the worst times'. In all of our world's history, there appears nothing so dastardly: a young man – still only in His vigorous, sensitive thirties – who had healed the sick, comforted the distraught, encouraged the dispirited, and taught the fullest revelation of God the world had ever seen – betrayed by one whom He trusted as friend; denied by another; falsely charged; lashed and ridiculed; stripped of His clothes; and hanged upon a Cross under the wide sky, with a crucified criminal for groaning companionship on either side!

True, a little handful of faithful friends – both men and women, even His mother – stood beneath that Cross, as close as they dared; the sun mingling hour after hour with their sorrow, beating down mercilessly. A cross, out beyond a city wall! One can never claim to understand everything involved in this stark event – and though we have sung about it for close on two thousand years, talked of it, written of it, and portrayed what in our deepest spirits we feel about it, making pictures for our homes, libraries, and galleries, and stained glass for our churches, we still don't feel we have plumbed the full meaning of the dread deed itself – the crown of thorns, the mockery, the forsakenness! But God was there, in that 'worst of times', hearing the words addressed to Him by that young man, His Son, Saviour of the world: 'Father, forgive them: for

116

they know not what they do!' (Luke 23:34, A.V.).

It is all too easy today, as we read our newspapers, to say 'the times are out of joint', as an excuse for turning from some essential piece of service. But the 'best', God-blessed thing can still be done in 'the worst of times', we know.

Maybe you too have read, as I have, *Wesley and His Century*, covering the religious and social darkness that was eighteenth-century England. 'But', quoting from that honest, rejoicing book treasured by many of us, 'what was coming to pass forms an epoch in English history.' One little clergyman with 'a warmed heart', was carrying away the heart of a people to give it to God. The judgement of subsequent secular historians is that God was again 'doing the best of things in the worst of times'.

And it's worth re-reading our social history books, with this in mind – to see how often it happens! I never go to London without going to the office and library of the British and Foreign Bible Society, that glorious centre of Life, serving an ever-increasing number of readers in every language in the world! And it started in the dark days of Napoleon's threat to overrun England!

I never cease to marvel! When you and I can get into perspective this 'doubtful' age in which we live, who can say we will not need to pause to fashion a like paean of praise?

> All my hope in God is founded;
>> He doth all my trust renew,
> Me through change and chance He guideth,
>> Only good and only true.
>>> God unknown,
>>> He alone
> Calls my heart to be His own.
>
> Joseph Neander

117

This World's Helpers

I love talking to children, and one of the best times is round the fire, after tea, in their own home. I shall always count myself richer for the night I spent in the home of David, Margaret and their little brother. After we'd shared a story, David suddenly came out with: 'Do you know what I'm going to be? A swimming teacher.' To that Margaret added: 'I'm going to be a nurse.'

'And what', I asked, 'is little Ian going to be?' Looking a little puzzled at first, he soon replied confidently: '*I'm going to be a helper*.' The bigger children laughed. But Ian will never be out of work, that's certain.

One of our modern-day poets, W. H. Auden, has underlined this beautifully: 'Ascribe it to prevenient grace, intuition, or sheer luck, one of the greatest things in any life has been the meeting with the right helper at the right time.'

A helper can be of any age, of either sex, and can exercise that gift for sheer love, or receive proper pay. It is what passes between giver and receiver that matters so much. Nobody knows, for certain, when the lovely designation first made its appearance – I guess it's as old as life. My Oxford Dictionary can only tie it to the archaic terms *holp* and *holpen*. But that doesn't get us very far. The next suggestion is that such a person is 'an assistant or companion to the mistress of a house'; and recognizing the limitations of that, we are soon moving on to 'helpmate', 'helpful companion or partner'.

That, to my thinking, suits very well what Paul meant in his lovely commendation to friends in Rome in one of his letters to them: 'Salute Urbane, our helper in Christ!' (Romans 16:9, A.V.). I've no idea how old he was, or what his skills – that doesn't seem to call for description in the New Testament. And there's good reason for that, since the New Testament is to last to this day, when forms of helpfulness are so changed. It was enough that Paul, the writer of that very human letter, should himself know the nature of that gift. As a simple matter of fact, I'd not even heard Urbane's name till I came upon it in this letter of Paul's. And for all my research since, I've not been able to find anything else about Urbane, save that his name (rendered 'Urbanus' in every version of Paul's letter, except the Authorized Version) is said to be a common one among servants in those days.

We don't read that Urbane ever preached, or taught, or took dictation from Paul on his journeys, or carried his bag. We don't know what form, or forms, his helping took. And it doesn't matter – from that day to this, opportunities presenting themselves to a 'helper' have been manifold.

Somebody has said: 'I would have been proud to have held the spyglass for Columbus; to have picked up his fallen brush for Michelangelo; to have carried Milton's bag; to have blacked Shakespeare's boots; or to have blown the organ-bellows for Handel.' Of course!

But God has some less famous, but scarcely less telling jobs going on! I came across one of them, a little while ago, remembered with gratitude, in Australia's little Kiama. I'd never heard of the little place, till I was invited there to speak to a company of people in the church, with its background of mountains and foreground of shimmering sea. I appreciated its countryness, but most of all, what I discovered about one of its 'helpers', a humble kinsman of Urbane.

Jim Crooks was his name, always to be remembered in little Kiama, though he has now long 'gone upon his way'.

119

He was the water-carrier. Day after day, he pushed on between the depleted house-tanks of the people and a soakage well, known with a chuckle as 'The Town Pump'. Often, as he passed to and fro, in the dry, hot seasons Australia knows, he must have recalled the well-watered, green England from which he had come. But he carried on at his water-carrying, patiently filling the two-hundred-gallon barrel mounted on cartwheels behind his old white horse. I wouldn't be at all surprised, if there were times when he wondered whether his plodding life was counting for anything. But now, in a lasting sense, there's no doubt at all: his memorial says he was 'a most successful Sunday School Teacher'.

I learned, to my amazement, that nine boys passed through his hands to become ministers of the Australian Church — four of them Presidents of the Methodist Conference, one, President General. When the gathering I had addressed dispersed, the kindly chairman took his pencil and copied down for me those nine names: 'William and Joseph Beale, William, Benjamin and John Dinning, Richard East, James Somerville, Dr R. N. Morris, and Dr J. E. Carruthers.' A fine and valiant company of whom, one by one, some scribe could have written – as did St Paul in his day – *thanks for a good helper!* A most successful Sunday School Teacher!

When I'm home, I go occasionally to a musical performance in the Town Hall. At one such evening, I had the pleasure of meeting and talking with Mr Paris. He was an usher on such occasions, and to regular concert-goers he became known as 'the man who lifted the lid of the piano'. He was not a performer himself, in the musical sense. But he was an unfailing performer at his helping.

My last morning newspaper, bridging the Old Year and the New, brought me the welcome but surprising news of old Mrs Lorna Hendrey. It began by saying that at first she could hardly believe the telegram that reached her, and I'm not surprised – this kind of thing doesn't happen very often. She – one of our humblest citizens – had been named in the New Year's Honours List! From time to time, we had all seen her about our streets, intent on her self-appointed task.

And what was that task? *Helping!* With her little trundler, she made her way from her home in nearby Milford, collecting empty bottles and broken glass. For years she had supervised bulk bottle collections by bottle companies. From the money raised, she had donated the sum of 4000 dollars to the Parklands Health Camp and the New Life Fellowship Group. In addition to this considerable sum, a further 3000 dollars was raised by old Mrs Hendrey for the North Shore Welfare Council. 'She was', the newspaper said, 'a familiar visitor to shops and businesses to collect bottles in her trundler. She also collected glass litter from beaches in the area.'

She had lived nearly all her life at Milford, until, some time back, she moved to a Rest Home a little further out. She now suffers from Parkinson's disease, and is, the paper said, 'unable to carry out her collections'. But what a fine piece of helpfulness! It was not only the charities which benefited from her years of help that gave thanks for her, but many of us who read of her being awarded the Queen's Service Medal.

Children often change with the years, of course, and little David might never become a swimming teacher, nor his sister, Margaret, a nurse; but I hope, with all my heart, that they will, all three, continue to be *God's good helpers in this world*!

Making Things

We may not be good at making things – a new dress, or a lawn at the front of the house – but most of us are good at making excuses.

It goes back a long way, of course. It's no use blaming Adam and Eve for it, although it is true that before ever they learned to make a well, a house, or a friendly relationship with other people, *they learned to make an excuse*. One of the early pages in our Bible gives us the story. They were in a garden when it happened: 'And they heard the sound of the Lord God walking in the Garden in the cool of the day. And the man and his wife hid themselves from the presence of the Lord God among the trees of the Garden. But the Lord God called to the man, and said to him, "Where are you?" And he said, "I heard the sound of Thee in the Garden, and I was afraid, because I was naked, and I hid myself." He said, "Who told you that you were naked? Have you eaten of the tree of which I commanded you not to eat?" The man said [and here come the world's first excuses], "The woman . . . she gave me fruit of the tree, and I ate" . . . The woman said, "The serpent beguiled me, and I ate"' (Genesis 3:8–13, R.S.V.). The man said 'the woman'; the woman said 'the serpent'; and so it has gone amongst us ever since, until the dictionary covering our language sets it down to this very day as '*the attempt to lessen the blame attaching to oneself*'; or in the second instance, '*to obtain exemption from some kind of service*'.

It is useless now to argue whether this ancient thumbnail sketch in Genesis is history or folklore. All that we know for sure is that in our experience an excuse comes in very handy at times – we are not often without one when we find ourselves in an embarrassing position. Pick up any newspaper with its report of Court news, or any novel reviewed at length in a favourite journal, and you'll find there in modern terms an echo of that first excuse. Or listen to the light song in which a young woman excuses her misdemeanours: 'It's not my fault. It's just my glands.' If this doesn't come off the tip of the tongue as readily as our need requires, it's easy to say: 'It's due to my heredity'; or, if that doesn't occur to us, 'to my early environment – we lived in the poor end of a little suburb, with no playgrounds'. Or if our family was well established, it's easy to say, 'My nurse dropped me out of my pram – she is to blame.' Apart from these, any first year college psychology textbook will very likely introduce the word 'libido', leading on to an example of emotional, even lustful craving, and we offer it as a sophisticated excuse for unwelcome behaviour.

If you have ever been called by your church to do house-to-house visiting in a new community where houses are going up, and the church stands already, you will have instances to share. And this is not to suggest that they are not found in long-established streets – they are. Sometimes it is just the weather: it's too wet, or too cold, or else too sunny 'to sit cooped up indoors for an hour on a lovely sunny morning'. As Principal Macgregor declared, rolling each word off his tongue, 'It takes an extraordinary concatenation of meteorological circumstances to make it possible for some people to come to church.' It still does!

Weather apart, some excuse themselves with a statement that they 'had too much church, as kids – twice a Sunday, with a dull preacher who had nothing to say to children', as they fiddled with hymnbooks, waiting to hear the Benediction pronounced.

Dame Ethel Smyth, of our day, speaks for those who don't look back to their childhood churchgoing. She says: 'At intervals we pray, but going to church bores us. Sometimes we think about Christ, but what with the films, the wireless, and a constant spate of detective novels, it is difficult to settle down to the New Testament.' (Weddings, funerals and baptisms, from time to time, they put into a separate category.)

Sometimes it is a matter of health, or it is easy to bring forward an excuse that embraces some members of the family. 'My husband can't go – he's so liable to colds – and I don't like to go without him. Sitting in a building that isn't *properly* warmed is no good to us.' There is every chance, of course, that he'll be better by tomorrow evening, when he goes to use a season ticket in the little theatre.

And there's the summer! But some fall back on their gardens to fashion an excuse, beautiful in their seasonal charms, even giving pleasure to passers-by, who stop to remark on them from time to time. But the weeds grow unbelievably, and there isn't much time in the week to get at them.

Another man – whose wife has kept her husband's churchgoing fairly constant when things are favourable, even to serving on some kind of committee that doesn't meet too often – suddenly announces that he is 'drawing out in favour of a younger man'. But this excuse has not occurred to him in relation to his golf club membership!

One of the very handiest of excuses is, of course, 'I am too busy.' Let a small child ask some long, involved question; or let some adult seek out one's help with some church or community project that is presently to the fore, and there is every chance that this excuse will be promptly offered.

There is no harm, of course, in being busy – some people really are. But it is being *over-busy* that spoils things, in

both worship and service – two experiences that we cannot
spare from this life of ours, if we put first values first, and
reach full satisfaction as our days go by. If it comes to that,
God has always used busy people. Young Moses was busy
at his daily shepherding on the back of the desert when God
called him to something else, something more exciting: the
leadership of his people. Gideon was busy on his threshing
floor, at one of the most crucial times of the whole season,
when his life-call came to him. Peter and Andrew, in New
Testament times, were overhauling their nets on their
familiar seashore, when the Lord of Life walked that way
– and called them with His words: 'Follow Me!' And all up
through the years it has been the same. A Christian knight
in the middle centuries was heard to pray: 'Lord, I shall be
verie busie this day. I may forget thee, but do not thou
forget me!' We don't hear any more of him; and we may
not hear any more of our *over-busy* committee colleague
as the years pass by, if it comes to that. Speaking for such
people, someone else says, by way of excuse: 'We are
driven here, there, and everywhere by the whirling
machinery of good works.'

Jesus told us a threefold, and very relevant story about
excuses. It had to do with a fine and important feast, to
which one by one the guests were invited (Luke 14:18–19,
A.V.). Surprisingly, although knowing our own hearts,
perhaps not so surprisingly – they each set out to make an
excuse. One had bought a field – a very worthwhile thing
to do, as were the undertakings of some other guests
invited. The man who had acquired the field, naturally
enough, wanted to go and have a look at it; the next, who
had bought himself a yoke of oxen, wanted to try them out;
and the third guest, who had, to his joyous wonder,
married a wife, felt that he couldn't get away at the
moment. But Jesus saw how their priorities stood, even to
the joy of possession; attention to better farming and travel

facilities; and the newly begun claims of affection. Not one of these undertakings could be properly dealt with in words, least of all, words of excuse! Priorities have to be reckoned with for what they are: priorities! It all depends, to this day, on what comes first! In this exciting, on-going life, '*making things*' *can be fun* – much more than making excuses – dresses and lawns perhaps, *as they serve the good Life we are here seeking*!

Never Anywhere Else

'Carl!' called the old garage owner, as I made my need known. It was a rattle that I didn't like, and wanted to be rid of. For several hours that morning, I'd travelled among the hills of that back area, and it might be miles before I came upon a more impressive garage. 'See what you can do for the lady', was the old man's next word, and I heard no more from him! Carl was almost as speechless. What he did say led me to ask: 'Where do you come from with a voice like that?' 'Poland!' he replied. 'How in the world did you get here?' 'Jumped ship!' said he. And that was the end of our conversation.

I often wonder about Carl, and did this morning when I read in my paper of sad days in his homeland. My brief meeting with him, and his small service rendered to me, came to mind when I turned a page and came to one that carried news of six other Polish men who had jumped ship. They were two radio operators, one steward, one motorman and two seamen. I had never heard of their vessel, the *Major Sucharski*. Where they are, by this time, I've no idea. All six were seeking official permission to stay, life for them in their own country having become intolerable.

I've never been to Poland, and know of it only from what I've read, and by its music. In the days of young Frederic Chopin, life was difficult enough, but in another way.

Frederic's mother, as you probably know, was a Polish lady, and like many of her people, she favoured music full of dances wild and memorable. His father came of French stock, and liked light, graceful music. Their young son, the musician, was only nine when he was first invited to play in homes, and sometimes he played in one mood, sometimes in the other.

In time, the young Pole needed to go from his village home into a fuller experience. Never would he forget the day when he clambered aboard a coach. Only one came that way, stopping long enough to change horses, and rest the weary passengers.

Through the liberality of Prince Antoine Radziwill, Chopin got to Warsaw college, and soon his youthful genius began to be recognized. On occasion he played to children gathered in their crowded schoolrooms – all too often undisciplined, enjoying noise and racket, with rulers and inkpots flying everywhere. Showing courage, young Frederic always spoke up, and said: 'I will not begin until there is quiet!'

The most important adult who summoned him to play was the Grand Duke Constantine, and at times he showed himself excited and brutal, too. Frederic's music always had the power of calming him. Thus, among the ordinary Polish people, his fame grew. During the following years, the adult Chopin visited city after city.

Then came a day when Poland was threatened by an invasion of the Russians, and Chopin was forced to flee his loved country. His friends and admirers gathered to give him a surprising parting present, one that to this moment I find fascinating. It was a little silver goblet, filled with ordinary Polish earth. The friend who handed it over said to sorrowing Frederic, Poland's now famous musician: 'May you never forget your homeland.' And from that time on, whenever and wherever he played, Chopin played with that little goblet of Polish earth set up on the piano before him, for a sign.

Now I sometimes find myself wondering if all is well with

Carl and with those six seamen who jumped ship at the port of the city where I live.

In the early days of the Old Testament, men forced to leave their native soil for a strange place carried with them a sizeable bag of the home soil. At those set times when they paused to pray to their fathers' God, they spread it out – and prayed upon it. Rapt in their devotions, they believed that God would bless them, as being *still upon their own soil*! There was young Jacob, for instance, fleeing after a family quarrel, when he had robbed his brother of his birthright. The only thing he could do was to run away.

When night came the young runaway – passionate, and utterly weary – could go no further. And in a strange, lonely place, he took for his pillow a stone, and threw himself down to sleep. In that moment home, and the God of Home, his father's God, seemed very far away.

But as he slept, he dreamed that 'a ladder set up on earth, reached to Heaven; and behold, the angels of God were ascending and descending on it! And behold, the Lord stood above it, and said, "I am the Lord, the God of Abraham your father and the God of Isaac; the land on which you lie I will give to you and to your descendants; and your descendants shall be like the dust of the earth, and you shall spread abroad to the west and to the east and to the north and to the south . . . *Behold, I am with you and will keep you wherever you go*, and will bring you back . . . for I will not leave you until I have done that of which I have spoken to you." Then Jacob awoke from his sleep and said, "Surely the Lord is in this place; and I did not know it"' (Genesis 28:16, R.S.V.).

The on-going march of Time since then has given us a growing assurance of that vital reality. We do not carry a bag of our home soil with us; the whole world is God's and *He can be found anywhere in it*. That's the meaning of the great religious term 'omnipresence', as applied to God our

Creator and Father. We know this, even more securely than did the Psalmist, years on after Jacob in his loneliness. His words underline that strengthening reality. Said the Psalmist, with splendid confidence: 'O Lord, Thou hast searched me, and known me. Thou knowest my downsitting and mine uprising, thou understandest my thought afar off. Thou compassest my path and my lying down, and art acquainted with all my ways . . . *Thou hast beset me behind and before, and laid Thine hand upon me. Such knowledge*', he finishes, '*is too wonderful for me; it is high, I cannot attain unto it. Whither shall I go from Thy spirit? Or whither shall I flee from Thy presence? If I ascend up into heaven, Thou art there: if I make my bed in hell, behold, Thou art there. If I take the wings of the morning, and dwell in the uttermost parts of the sea; even there shall Thy hand lead me, and Thy right hand shall hold me*' (Psalm 139:1–10, A.V.). All places to Him are equally near, and equally far off. No member of His human earth-family is outside His presence.

Much nearer our own time, the young students gathered to listen to Lord Moynihan, the great British surgeon, had a chance to learn this. As well as lecture, Lord Moynihan was asked from time to time to operate before a group of them. At the end of one such demonstration, one young doctor spoke up: 'It must be very difficult for you to operate before a group of young surgeons watching your every move.' There was a pause, but only for a few seconds; then Lord Moynihan said: 'It is like this: there are just three people in the theatre when I operate – the patient and myself.'

'Three?' asked the questioner. 'But that is only two; who is the other?'

The great surgeon answered quietly: 'God!'

And that is true for any of us – for Carl; for six of his countrymen far from home, where they jumped ship; for you and me – a lonely distance from home, or lonely at home, even lonely in church. On a certain Monday morning, the great Old Testament scholar, Professor Adam Welch, startled his students with new words that they had never heard before in the quiet of Opening Prayer. One of them, Dr James S. Stewart, later admitted: 'I suppose he was becoming restive listening to so many student prayers beginning with the stereotyped phrase: "O God, we come into Thy presence." At any rate this day the prayer began, "O God, we do *not* come into Thy presence", then a lengthened pause, and then, "*for we are never anywhere else*".'

Isn't Good Talk Good!

The hour was late when I got to the glowing hearth of my friends, the winter sky, under which we walked, gemmed with stars. It had been a long day, ending with a meeting and an open forum, and I was glad to relax.

Ormond drew in three deep chairs, and his wife went to bring in the supper. 'Once in a while,' as Logan Pearsall Smith has said, 'when doors are closed and curtains drawn on a group of free spirits, the miracle happens, and *good talk begins*.'

Experts tell us that the average word-flow of most of us each day, before night calls us to rest, is twenty thousand words. It seems a great many to me, and put down like that, it fails to suggest the subtle secret of enrichment. There was no need, at any rate, to count words as we three sat together before that fire. In between eager talk, there were instants of complete silence – and when next somebody spoke, it was plain that all were thinking along the same lines.

Before the sun had found its way through the gaps in the hills nearby next morning, I was on my way to the airport. A day or two later, at home, I received a letter from that comfortable old manse, which said: 'I do hope our paths cross again. *Isn't good talk good!*'

It is! Despite some words I hadn't met before, words that jumped off the page, challengingly, as I read in the Book of Proverbs, where I don't often turn to read. In chapter 18 verse 21 (R.S.V.) it said: '*Death and Life are in the power of the tongue.*' (No mention of the number of words, but a statement sundered straight down the middle, between Death and Life! So one might say a great deal on one side or the other. The Book of Proverbs, of course, is not the work of one mind, but the collection of many persons, part of what the Bible calls 'the Wisdom Literature of Israel'.)

Since we are each one of us blessed with a tongue, these wise words from the dawn of Time ought to have something of worth to say to us. These, one had to accept, were words still relevant! I found them worth learned and lengthy comment in *The Interpreter's Bible* of our modern, noisy, gossiping century.

Curiously – though it had no place in our evening before the fire – the word 'gossip' has changed with the years. It started into the life of our forebears as 'God-sib', meaning a person who stood supportingly, beside one in baptism, during infancy. But somewhere, during the on-going centuries, it degenerated into the word we have today, 'gossip'. Nevertheless, for a long while, it continued with a rather pleasant connotation, as 'a familiar acquaintance, a friend'. It did not at once become the nasty little word it is today – what the dictionary calls 'an idle talker, a news-monger, a tattler'.

But by the time Dr Moffatt, followed by Dr Weymouth and the translators of our Revised Standard Version, came to give us Paul's New Testament Letter to young Timothy, his colleague, the little word 'gossip' had appeared. He had something pertinent to say about 'younger widows . . . who learn to be idlers, gadding about from house to house, and not only idlers but *gossips* and busybodies saying what they should not' (1 Timothy 5:12,13, R.S.V.). It is an unhappy picture, the more so when today we have no assurance that this damaging use of the tongue is restricted to those mentioned by Paul, within the community of his day.

Edmund Gosse – not a 'younger widow', of course, but a gifted author nearer our time – is an unforgettable case.

There was no doubt about his being a gossip. Even his kindly biographer, Evan Charteris, had to admit as much. 'Gosse', he wrote, 'had the weakness, as all his friends knew, of saying one thing in a letter, and quite another thing in conversation . . . Mr Brighteyes would send Gosse his new book, with a little letter of a friendly and properly submissive tone. And Gosse, whose heart was always of the warmest, who, moreover, was for ever needing reassurance from *his* friends, would write a most complimentary letter in return, saying that he had found the book a proper masterpiece. But in gay and merry after-dinner conversation, that same book would be mentioned, and out would come Gosse's claw – the witty thing would be said, and next day would be repeated!'

'Happy are they who converse', said Tertullian, the early Christian theologian, *'as those who know that God hears.'* His words have been preserved over the centuries, since he felt moved to give them to the world which daily knew the talk of fine men and women, and not only of the 'younger widows' who bothered Paul so much. Plainly, Edmund Gosse had not come upon his telling words – or if he had, had decided they were of no consequence to him. But whoever we are, and wherever we are, surely no one of us can claim exception.

In our day, a woman confesses as much in a chance talk with an acquaintance, after some damage has been done. 'She told me', said she, 'that you told her the secret I told you not to tell her.' 'Oh, the mean thing!' came the all-too-ready retort, 'I told her not to tell you I had told her!' Gossip is not always as involved as that – but it can be.

One is glad to pass on to the second part of our proverb: 'Death and Life', it says, 'are in the power of the tongue.' We have instanced a case of causing the death of glad,

134

strong, enjoyable acquaintance. But there is the other half
of the proverb that led my friend to write to me, after we
three had left behind us that night our glowing fire: 'Isn't
good talk good!' We love to talk of people of the past, who
have inspired us; and of the present, with whom we share
so much of our on-going life in this world. And thus talk
can carry life not death! We need it – call it 'gossip' if you
like – but it is 'gossip reclaimed', without bitterness and
ugliness and spite. At its heart is life!

Do you remember the strengthening experience of John
Bunyan? The dissolute soldier-tinker of Bedford early one
morning chanced upon a little handful of 'gossips'. It was
at a time when he was far from pleased with his way of life
and was badly conscience-stricken. What he heard that
morning helped him greatly. They 'gossiped', he reported
– pausing within hearing distance – *of the greatest things of
life that were to be had, within the Love of God*! And
Bunyan laid hold of them for himself by faith, and became
one of the greatest Christians of the day.

We could do as much, of course – we don't have to be
preachers, theological students, religious writers, just
ordinary people of faith. One great missionary of our day,
Mildred Cable, whom I had the pleasure of meeting both
in London and in my own country, after her return from
incredible journeys across the Gobi Desert, and parts of
China and Russia. She spoke in her public addresses of
little groups of people, in unexpected places. 'And what
were they doing?' she was continually asked. Her answer
was always striking: *'They were gossiping Communism
across the country!'*

And what's to stop us modern-day Christians doing the
same – *in the most gracious way we know* – 'gossiping
the gospel'? 'In the glorious days of missionary expansion,
following the death of Paul, the real work', says Dr E. F.
Scott, 'was done by countless obscure men and women who

135

made it their first duty to spread the message in their own circle of friends and neighbours.' They weren't apostles, preachers, or even members of evangelization committees, but men and women of Living Faith who, *in the most gracious way they knew*, witnessed to Christ, their Redeemer and Lord! I have purposely italicized twice over this hint about being *gracious*, in this daily ministry to which we are called. It is of such importance – nothing can take its place. Links with others are very often built on fragile bridges of respect, admirable character, and warm reality.

A City Drew Him

Those of us born and brought up in the lush green of the countryside, may question to our life's end why people ever long to live in cities. Yet they do – and tell of it as a rich experience. And some who in maturity visit cities, are just as enthusiastic. Away back in AD 63, when Tacitus, earliest of foreign correspondents, spent some time in Roman London, he spoke of it as 'celebrated for the gathering of dealers and commodities'. I wonder what he would say today? He might, of course, make the same mistake as I made myself, when first I fell in love with one, by thinking of the whole conglomerate of buildings great and small, ancient and new, as London. Two or three centuries ago, it might have been as simple as that. But now, there is no *one* London – the City of London, surprisingly, is that Square Mile within the wall of Roman days. People pour into that area daily, but hardly anybody sleeps there save the Lord Mayor, and an army of caretakers and cats.

A great part of what we look upon, as visitors, is the County of London, that comprises – apart from the City – twenty-eight boroughs embracing well nigh seventy-six thousand acres. And there is Greater London, the Metropolitan Police area – six times larger than the County – covering the whole of Middlesex, and reaching out to embrace the most thickly populated suburbs of Surrey, Kent, Hertfordshire and Essex. Apart from miles and miles of streets, and countless buildings, the great city has some thousands of acres of docks. Boswell believed that London 'comprehended the whole of human life in its variety'. And that is now truer than ever. What a city!

Sometimes it is open to spring – and a lovelier natural surprise of budding trees, green lawns, bursting crocuses and daffodils and bluebells cannot be found anywhere the world round. But there are other times, when bitterly cold, sleety rain falls; and there have been yet others, when fog prevented its inhabitants from seeing not only its stately buildings, of which there are a great many, but also with any clarity the street a couple of on-going steps ahead. And I remember no more bewildering experience than to be guided across a completely befogged intersection by a policeman – who at first appeared as a blur.

But one forgets fog, smog, and strap-hanging in the Underground at rush-hours. For always there is something old, and something new, to see in London. One morning, as I stood watching one of London's spectacles, the Changing of the Guard, take place a few steps from me, I overheard a little boy – amazed at the soldiers' beautiful scarlet and gold uniforms, their tall black busbies, and meticulous movements – ask his father, tugging at his hand, 'Daddy, are they *real* men inside?' That is the question that springs often to one's lips in London, when one is fortunate enough to see what she can do, in the way of processions, and displays, and royal happenings.

Outside London, I am thankful to have visited many other English cities. I was in busy Coventry before the war, when the old Cathedral stood; and later, and gladly, have worshipped in the new Cathedral. Always I marvel at the two Christly words not to be missed as one comes to the old altar: 'FATHER FORGIVE!'

Canon Stephen Verney served as Director of Studies for the 'People and Cities' conference one year when I was in Coventry, and followed it up with a paperback book from my publishers, Collins. His first sentence is: 'This . . . is about the urgent problem now confronting the human race

– what is happening to *people*, as all over the world they crowd into bigger and bigger cities?' And under its first chapter heading is a startling quotation to which we must all give some Christian attention if that, by the mercy of Christ, is within our power. '*In the modern city*', says the quotation from Professor Hare, after that important conference on 'People and Cities' had finished, '*hate between rich and poor, rulers and ruled, is much easier to preach than love; but unless love is both preached and most skilfully practised, our cities will fall apart.*'

And where do we get this great quality of Love? – from none other than Christ Himself, who wept over Jerusalem, His own most-loved City.

> A city drew Him.
> Flowers He found in little children's eyes;
> Something of grace in lepers stumbling to Him;
> Fragrance from spikenard spilt in glad surprise;
> Joy in forgiving men at last who slew Him;
> Courage in service, hope in sacrifice.

In a handbook on *Journalism*, that I brought as its first reader from the library today, I was arrested by one paragraph: 'More than one older journalist has commended to the notice of his younger colleagues the most affecting sentence in literature: "Jesus wept"' (John 11:35, A.V.). It is the shortest verse in the New Testament – but it is one that needs long thinking about by those who live in cities. And I live on the rim of one myself!

This challenge rises before me every time I recall my own visit to Jerusalem. I got a ride to the topmost area of the city, that afforded me a perfect view, and quietness. Then I walked down a narrow, winding ankle-breaking street, past the entrance of the Garden of Gethsemane. On the way, I paused at a little chapel, still high up, known as

139

Dominus Flevit (Jesus Wept). Those words, set there for all passers-by to see, represent manly grief deeper than any known before. On entering the chapel, I found beyond the altar, engraved on its glass, His chalice, and other symbols of His sacrificial Love, and I saw the whole city He knew and loved, spread out.

Our world holds more cities than ever today, many of them reaching up to the skies.

And so I came back home, in time, to my own city on the other side of the world, with a timely prayer on my lips:

> Christ, look upon me in this city,
> And keep my sympathy and pity
> Fresh, and my face heavenward;
> Lest I grow hard. AMEN.

Preparing For Christmas

Sometimes Christmas seems a long way off and then suddenly it's not! Because of the International Date Line Christmas Day comes first to Tonga, with joyous notes of the church bell ringing out early, and the people gathering to worship. So it is fitting to call those islands 'The Kingdom of the Dawn'.

When for five weeks I was guest of the late beloved Queen Salote in order to speak to her people, I was taken at once to see the big church near the palace. I was surprised that it could comfortably hold two thousand people, white-clad, stepping gently, coming in to sing, to listen, and to pray. And I was sincerely moved to be told that, not counting the Queen, I was the first churchwoman to be invited to ascend those pulpit steps, to lead worship and praise.

The spacious floor all about the pulpit was finely covered with handwoven matting, with beautiful patterns. And as I approached the lower steps on the first day, I saw three words that I had not met before: KUO KE TEUTEU. I asked about them, and was told what they meant – words of great significance for a leader of worship: *'Have you prepared?'*

At that point, I knew that those words meant something more than 'Have you a good sermon?' It was too late, if by any chance I hadn't. And I knew they were not asking, 'Is your message theologically sound?' 'And is it tellingly and persuasively expressed?' It was a bit late if I had not prepared, for to be prepared was all-important. And I knew it meant something much deeper, something out of my long-time Christian Faith and practical experience, nothing less than *a vital, rejoicing preparation of mind and spirit*. It was a challenge.

And I want to ask the same question as Christmas approaches: '*Have you prepared?*' And I don't mean just bringing out the Christmas tree; icing the cake; sending innumerable greeting cards; checking the guest list; counting up gifts for the children, having regard to their ages; bringing in extra chairs on the day, for grandparents and neighbours one seldom sees. All these things can matter, and can be counted part of the preparation for weeks beforehand, adding up to a kind of lightsome jollity. But it is not that alone!

The word '*prepare*' appears all through the Old and New Testaments. (Take out your Concordance, and you'll find how constantly God used this lovely word when He set about sending us His Son – *which is what Christmas means*!) When Paterson Smyth wrote for my generation *A People's Life of Christ*, he began there with the chapter 'A World Preparing'.

More clearly than anyone I know, he sets out the tremendous preparation that God did to offer this world of ours His Son. 'At last', he begins, 'the time drew near. And as it came, behold a marvellous thing. *The world beginning to make ready . . .*

'Here are the facts. When the Christ was coming, three races held the chief influence – the Greek, the Roman, and the Jew . . . No others mattered. First, the Roman made *the road for the coming of the King*. A century before Messiah's day, the world was intensely localized and sub-divided and broken up into separate little nations, with their separate religions and customs and laws, their jealousies and suspicions, their constant wars, their bristling frontiers barring communications. The land was harassed by skirmishing bands, the sea was impassable by reason of pirates. Humanly speaking, a century before Christ, no Palestine movement could ever have spread beyond Palestine. It was humanly impossible for a universal Gospel' when Jesus came to give it, and to His disciples spoke, saying: 'Ye shall be witnesses unto Me both in Jerusalem, and in all Judaea [further out] and in Samaria [further still] *and unto the uttermost part of the earth*' (Acts 1:8, A.V.). He couldn't have spoken to them in this way without the contribution of the great road-making Romans!

Paterson Smyth says, with wonder and thankfulness: 'Just at this crisis came a striking change . . . when Jesus came, instead of frontiered nations separated and suspicious, He found a levelled world with the fences down. Rome had welded the incoherent kingdoms into one, smashing up the separated patriotisms and religions, federating the world into a single great monarchy. The Roman roads traversed the civilized world, the iron power of the Caesars kept universal peace. One has but to watch the free, unrestricted journeys of St Paul all over the Empire to see what the Roman peace and the Roman road and the Roman world unity meant to the spread of the new religion.'

What a preparation that was! All essential for the coming of the Gospel of Christ, and a messenger beforehand! The word 'prepare' first appears, in the New Testament, in connection with John the Baptist (Matthew 11:10, A.V.). 'I send My messenger before Thy face, which shall prepare Thy way before Thee.' It was no simple matter to John the Baptist, born, grown, and out on his special ministry, completing the first wonder of the first Christmas, leading on to the first wonder of Christ's Gospel!

This word 'prepare' keeps running in the mind – as it must!

God had next to use men to prepare *a universal language*

to carry His Gospel along those great roads. And it was the second people, the word-loving Greeks, who did that. For centuries God had been preparing them. 'The Jews spoke Aramaic,' as Paterson Smyth reminds us in his chapter 'A World Preparing', 'the Romans knew Latin, the many peoples spoke languages as confused as Babel. But as the day drew near when Messiah was coming, the Greek, all unknowing, was doing his part to prepare the way of the Lord.

'His beautiful, flexible tongue became the chief language of the Empire. Men all round the Mediterranean, while speaking their own language, also learned to use Greek. It became the language of the whole civilized world. Thus the vehicle was prepared for carrying the new teaching.' It wouldn't have been any advantage to have the Roman roads stretching to the four corners of the known world, waiting for the footsteps of missionaries, and the new world-redeeming Gospel they carried, if beyond that they shared no universally understood language, over and above their own little local dialects.

But God did not overlook this essential element of preparation – along the wide, Roman roads, conquering the miles, could now stride missionaries with Christ's Gospel. Greek was what was called 'a tongue understanded of the people'. Never were any who shared it more proud than of their beautiful tongue! Never was any people more glad of their culture, and both, thanks to the loving and far-sighted preparation of God's purpose, were baptized into the on-going centuries.

Today, the message of the Gospel has proved how communicable this living Word of the Kingdom of Christ is, now handed from one to another in type, translated from the original Greek, so that our Bible Societies are always expanding the round figures of its world triumph!

And the third people were the Jews. One of the most

telling verses in the New Testament rejoices in it: 'When the fulness of Time was come, *God sent forth His Son, made of a woman, made under the Law, to redeem*' (Galatians 4:4, A.V.).

The countdown of the first Christmas of this world was the longest, most deliberately planned operation in all Time. Following on the contribution of the Romans and the Greeks, we come to that of the Jews, who through the centuries kept alive in their spirits the expectation of God's richest revelation: the gift of His Son. And in the fulness of Time, He came! 'The Incarnation began', said Warburton Lewis to us, 'when Mary said, "Into Thy hands I commend my body"; the Incarnation was "finished" when her Son said, "Into Thy hands I commend My spirit".' 'In the sixth month the angel Gabriel was sent from God to a town in Galilee called Nazareth, with a message for a girl betrothed to a man named Joseph, a descendant of David; the girl's name was Mary. The angel went in and said to her, "Greetings, most favoured one! The Lord is with you!" And she was deeply troubled by what he said, and wondered what this greeting might mean. Then the angel said to her, "Do not be afraid, Mary, for God has been gracious to you; you shall conceive and bear a son, and you shall give Him the name Jesus"' (Luke 1:26–31, N.E.B.).

And so the world heard a new song as Mary sang:

Tell out, my soul, the greatness of the Lord,
rejoice, rejoice, my spirit, in God my saviour;
so tenderly has He looked upon His servant,
    humble as she is.
For, from this day forth,
all generations will count me blessed,
so wonderfully hath He dealt with me,
    the Lord, the Mighty One!

And the song lengthened, as the wonder of it grew (Luke 1:46–55, N.E.B.). So was given to the world its first Christmas: the little Son of God, born at the close of Mary's nine months of womanly patience.

Postscript

I never dreamed that between writing the chapter you have just read, and celebrating the glad Christmas festival itself, having submitted my book-in-the-making to my publishers in London, I would be writing a new ending to my book. But here it is!

Before I could be asked to write the usual contract for that book, or Christmas could find me, came a happening totally unexpected. Not that the reality of my carefully chosen title, and what I had written under it, had lost any of its reality – not at all – not least the prayer with which I started out: '*God, help me to be continually aware!*'

When a dear book-friend in Canada learned of Rene's death, she wrote: 'Because she was so much part of your life, she is also a part of your writing and the joy it gives to others. For all who knew her personally, and for those who, like myself, came to know her through the written word, her spirit will continue to give "a lovely light".' Then she added, very sensitively: 'I cannot wish you a merry Christmas, but I wish you its peace, and the comfort of that Love of which all our dearest loves are an imperishable part.'

Many cards came, as Christmas approached, but no one more tellingly summed up its reality for me. And now I sit to add this postscript to the book which I never, even after a number of people had suggested it to me at the close of her Service at St George's, thought to do. But, as the weeks pass, and I have dealings with my considerate publishers, it seems right that I should ask whether I might delete my concluding chapter, and put this one in its stead. It was Rene, after all, who fifty-one years ago – in unwavering friendship, with house-sharing, travel and work – first suggested that I should write, in the fashion in which I had hitherto spoken to many people in many places. And this was the last of many manuscripts she was with me to read. My book immediately before it – *Discoveries That Delight*, on 'a fresh love of the Psalms' – carried the words: 'Dedicated to My Home-sharing Friend, Rene.' She was a warm, strong character – and a very dear one.

One morning early, she suffered a fall down some steps, and struck her head on a piece of concrete, breaking her skull in two places. Doctor, nurse, and ambulance lost no time in getting her into the Intensive Care Unit of our City Hospital. She was unable to speak for a long period, or to see or hear. I went to her bedside ninety-one of the ninety-four days she was in hospital altogether, thanks to the wonderful care of a handful of church friends – men and women – who motored me to and from the Hospital some miles off, every afternoon without fail.

We feared that her brain might be damaged, when days went by in silence, though I always spoke on approaching her bed. It was thought that my familiar voice might be a helpful link with normality. It may well have been so, as is often the case with deeply unconscious folk. But many days passed.

Then one late afternoon, as I was coming away, she suddenly said, in a normal speaking voice, 'Thank you for your love!' I was greatly cheered, and phoned my good motorist-friends that night, to share the hopeful news.

But a great many more days passed without further communication. Then, once more, as I was leaving, she spoke again, and at some length, in her normal voice: 'Are

148

you getting good meals?' 'Yes,' I was able to reply, 'my friends are very kind to me. And when I don't go out to share a meal with them, not missing a single day, I boil up my pot of vegetables and get meat, and stew some kind of fruit for dessert. Of course,' I added, 'its not an eight-dollar dinner, like you put on.' At that, she gave a little chuckle, and said, 'I have yet to see the eight dollars!' I went on: 'You will, you will!' Then she lowered her voice, and added: 'Forget about it, forget about it! Anything that I've ever been able to do for you through the years, I've been well recompensed for – you're so appreciative!'

I moved away from her bed stepping on air – but she was never again to speak like that, at such length, and with such long words. And very early on the morning of the ninety-fourth day, the little hospital nearer home where she was now being carefully tended, rang me that she was not so well. I found her again deeply unconscious. But as I spoke to her, she opened her eyes widely and looked straight at me – then gently nestled into her pillow, and in a matter of moments was 'gone upon her way'.

It was merciful – I knew. I did not need the doctor, or the nursing sister to assure me of that. She could not have recovered her happy, active life, here.

On the Saturday morning, neighbours, relations and friends gathered in her beloved St George's Presbyterian Church for a Service of Thanksgiving. Led by her minister, the readings were shared by a close ministerial friend, until lately Assistant Minister of St George's. And a striking and helpful Tribute was paid by a beloved Methodist minister, a friend of many years, the Rev. Ashleigh Petch. He said:

'Irene Watts – Rene, as she was known to family and close friends – had a very useful and rewarding life. As the only daughter in the family of James, the banker, and his wife Elizabeth, at Onehunga, she was born in the family apartment of the Onehunga Branch of the Auckland Savings Bank, becoming one of the early depositors, seeing that her father registered her at birth, in "the penny bank".

'But Rene received more important benefits from the home in which she grew up. She had the advantage of a good education – following her years at the local Primary School, she attended the city's Girls' Grammar School, at a time when secondary education was not regarded as essential for young women. Throughout her life, she was an avid reader, a perceptive thinker, and a stimulating conversationalist. Furthermore,' he was happy to add, 'she absorbed Christian standards which stood her in good stead throughout her life. Self-discipline was important to her – self-respect, consideration for others, integrity, tolerance, friendliness and large-heartedness – qualities which, along with her wry sense of humour, won for her the confident respect of all with whom she had to do. Balanced in outlook, tolerant always, gracious in disposition, she was also seen to be courageous in adversity, as the years passed.

'Her people were originally Congregationalists, but because of the absence of young people in that particular congregation, they moved to the neighbouring Presbyterian Church – and there served in the choir, the Sunday School, and, as Rene grew, in youth leadership – in what was known throughout the country from end to end as the Bible Class Movement. In time she became, for many years, the secretary of the Movement, many times a leader at Youth Conferences, occasionally a speaker. Along with their shared Faith, developed many friendships.

'It was partly through a cousin, Sister Lena Button, a Tasmanian Methodist Deaconess, that Rene came to meet her closest friend, Rita Snowden, who was, herself, a well-known Methodist Deaconess at the time, and who had trained along with her cousin, Lena, at Deaconess House in Christchurch. When Rita moved to work in the northern city, she boarded for some time with the Watts family – as it was after Mr Watts's death, and shared it with Rene, after her mother's death – until later, the two young women bought a section at Titirangi, in the distant range behind the city – themselves cleared the wild growth, saved selected trees, and built their home, "West Hills", whose doors for sixteen years were open to many in hospitality and friendship.

'Thus was developed between them a friendship which has grown and deepened over some fifty-one years, bringing immeasurable enrichment, not only to each other, but also to friends far and near, in New Zealand and beyond. It has been a remarkable friendship, so wholesome and strong, in which individuality has blossomed and each has been free to be herself. As Rita', he went on, 'put it to me only yesterday, as I assembled some facts of Rene's early life, for this Tribute, "We haven't pushed each other around". Rene had her music teaching, and Rita her writing and speaking. Rene trained in her homeland, acquiring her letters, and established herself as a teacher of note who sought and achieved high standards. On her first visit to England, with her friend in 1937, she took a course at the Tobias Matthay School of Teaching in London, and on her return, became an exponent of his methods. She would begin her teaching as early as seven each morning – teaching not only children and young people, but also adults, men and women – some professional people, some budding music teachers themselves – and as time passed, reaching out to children of her early pupils . . .

'In her autobiography, *The Sun is High*, Rita quotes

from a friend's letter: "I feel that you and Rene have made something very wonderful out of your friendship. You are each so different, yet each so much herself . . . Another thing is that you are so outreaching towards the rest of us . . . Of course, you've had the fun of knowing each other's friends all the while; and because you haven't conformed to a pattern, you've kept each other fresh. So that when I'm in your home, I feel that there is a healthy wind blowing. I am sure its secret lies somewhere within that phrase you once coined for me when we spoke about friendship: 'We are bonded together in a sweet liberty.'"

'. . . Rene's outlook was broadened and enriched by travel. On three occasions she joined Rita in overseas visits for almost twelve months at a time. And through the years, along with Rita, she maintained through correspondence, contact with their overseas friends.

'Yet life had for both its dark and difficult days. Rene endured nine surgical operations – two for cancer – but faced them with quiet courage, and the serenity born of Faith. Just as in earlier years, she had nursed her friend through two years of grievous heart trouble, so Rita supported her in shadowed, as well as in sunny hours. All through the journey together they have cared for and supported each other. It was in these times of critical illness that Rene found much in the Psalms, and especially in Psalm 23, the Shepherd Psalm. It was not for naught that the hymns noted in the back of her book were "Praise, my soul, the King of Heaven!" and "The Lord's my Shepherd". There was a time, some years ago, when marooned by a phenomenal storm, at Quentin Hut on the Milford Track, the small company gathered around the piano – it being Sunday . . . A young woman played the piano until someone asked for "The Lord's my Shepherd", to the tune "Crimond" which had been made popular by its use in the wedding service of our Queen Elizabeth and

Prince Philip. A copy of it could not be found, so in the end, Rene quietly said, "Perhaps I could play it, as it is one I know from memory". And play it she did, to the great joy of a hitherto unnoticed Scotsman, one of the sheltering Track-keepers, who at that moment had stepped out of the cookhouse, and joined in the singing of the Psalm.

'It is fitting, therefore,' finished our friend, 'that this Psalm be sung in this service of Thanksgiving and farewell. It voices the deep, sturdy faith in God and in our Lord Jesus Christ which sustained Rene throughout her life's journey – a faith free from sentimentality. It seems so appropriate that Rita's latest book *Discoveries That Delight* – a book on the Psalms – should contain the following words: "Dedicated to My Home-sharing Friend, Rene."

'We rejoice because of the home into which Rene was born, and whose faith and values she came to share. We rejoice because of the home she, with Rita, established and adorned, and in whose life and mainstay she so richly shared. We rejoice also that for Rene, so utterly Christian, the adventure of death was simply a going home to share the richer, fuller life, the ampler air . . . Thanks be to God!'

RENE

On a fresh morning
   in spring
She went upon her way,
   calmly,
Her work here
   finished,
Her faith gloriously
   supporting.

               R.F.S.

Acknowledgements

The author acknowledges with gratitude the use of material from the following works. Other quotations are brief, out of copyright, or fully acknowledged in the script.

Chirgwin, A. M., *The Bible in World Evangelism*, SCM Press, 1954, p. 12.

Crossly-Holland, Kevin, *Pieces of Land*, Victor Gollancz.

Farjeon, Eleanor, 'Morning has broken', anthology, Michael Joseph.

Farmer, H. H., sermon quoted in *Life and Work*, Church of Scotland.

Kay, J. Alan, *The Wise Design*, Epworth Press.

Kennedy, Gerald, *I Believe*, Abingdon Press, USA, pp. 22–3.

Manson, T. W., *Ministry and Priesthood*, p. 21.

Paterson Smyth, J., *A People's Life of Christ*, Hodder and Stoughton, People's Library Edition, 1921, p. 20.

Pellow, John, article in *The British Weekly*.

Phillips, J. B., *Your God is Too Small*, Epworth Press, London.

Pilkington, Roger, *Heavens Alive*, Macmillan & Co, 1964.

Read, David H. C., 'It Sometimes Happens . . . ' from *I Am Persuaded*.

Snowden, Rita F., 'On My Two Feet!' was first published in *The Upper Room*, Abingdon Press, and is used by kind permission of the Editor.

Snowden, Rita F., 'Preparing for Christmas' was first published in *The Methodist Recorder*, London.

Whitham, A. E., sermons reprinted in *The Catholic Christ*, Hodder and Stoughton, 1940, p. 42.

Also available in Fount Paperbacks

BOOKS BY RITA SNOWDEN

More Prayers for Women

'. . . she has that rare and valuable gift of being able to compose forms of prayer which really do express the aspirations of many people . . .'

Philip Cecil, Church Times

Prayers for Busy People

'. . . her collection of prayers have the mark of sincerity and relevance.'

Crusade

Prayers for the Family

'. . . For those who have wanted to make a start with family prayers and have not quite known how to begin, this book offers the opportunity and a method.'

Expository Times

Also available in Fount Paperbacks

BOOKS BY RITA SNOWDEN

Bedtime Stories and Prayers

A delightfully illustrated selection of prayers and true stories for children at bedtime.

Christianity Close to Life

'Her great concern is to show how practical the life of faith . . .'
Neville Ward, Church Times

I Believe Here and Now

'Once again she has produced for us one of the most readable and helpful pieces of Christian witness I have seen . . .'
D. P. Munro, Life and Work

A Woman's Book of Prayers

'This book will make prayer more real and meaningful for all who use it. There is all through the book an accent of reality. Here the needs of the twentieth century are brought to God in twentieth century language.'

William Barclay

Fount Paperbacks

Fount is one of the leading paperback publishers of religious books and below are some of its recent titles.

- ☐ DISCRETION AND VALOUR (New edition)
  Trevor Beeson   £2.95 (LF)
- ☐ ALL THEIR SPLENDOUR David Brown   £1.95
- ☐ AN APPROACH TO CHRISTIANITY
  Bishop Butler   £2.95 (LF)
- ☐ THE HIDDEN WORLD Leonard Cheshire   £1.75
- ☐ MOLCHANIE Catherine Doherty   £1.00
- ☐ CHRISTIAN ENGLAND (Vol. 1)
  David Edwards   £2.95 (LF)
- ☐ MERTON: A BIOGRAPHY Monica Furlong   £2.50 (LF)
- ☐ THE DAY COMES Clifford Hill   £2.50
- ☐ THE LITTLE BOOK OF SYLVANUS
  David Kossoff   £1.50
- ☐ GERALD PRIESTLAND AT LARGE
  Gerald Priestland   £1.75
- ☐ BE STILL AND KNOW Michael Ramsey   £1.25
- ☐ JESUS Edward Schillebeeckx   £4.95 (LF)
- ☐ THE LOVE OF CHRIST Mother Teresa   £1.25
- ☐ PART OF A JOURNEY Philip Toynbee   £2.95 (LF)

All Fount paperbacks are available at your bookshop or newsagent, or they can also be ordered by post from Fount Paperbacks, Cash Sales Department, G.P.O. Box 29, Douglas, Isle of Man, British Isles. Please send purchase price, plus 10p per book. Customers outside the U.K. send purchase price, plus 12p per book. Cheque, postal or money order. No currency.

NAME (Block letters) _____

ADDRESS _____

_____

_____